Stadium Stories:

Nebraska Cornhuskers

Stadium Stories™ Series

Stadium Stories:

Nebraska Cornhuskers

Colorful Tales of the Scarlet and Cream

Mike Babcock

The Globe Pequot Press

GUILFORD, CONNECTICUT

Stadium Stories is a trademark of Morris Book Publishing, LLC.

Text design: Casey Shain

Cover photos courtesy of UNL Photography (top right, middle right,
bottom left) and Huskers Illustrated (top left, middle left, bottom right)

Library of Congress Cataloging-in-Publication Data
Babcock, Mike.
   Stadium stories : Nebraska Cornhuskers : colorful tales of the
scarlet and cream / Mike Babcock.–1st ed.
      p. cm. – (Stadium stories series)
   ISBN 0-7627-3429-9
   1. University of Nebraska–Lincoln–Football–History. 2. Nebraska
Cornhuskers (Football team)–History. I. Title: Nebraska Cornhuskers.
II. Title. III. Series.
GV958.U53B334 2004
796.332'63'09782293–dc22   2004054271

Manufactured in the United States of America
First Edition/First Printing

To my parents, Bab and Dorothy, for their unconditional love and unwillingness to acknowledge my limitations; my brother, Jim, for remaining my best friend despite the miles that separate us; my children, Chad and Heather, for allowing their father to be gone at important times while growing up; and my wife, Barb, for her tolerance, constant support, and love.

Contents

Acknowledgments

What I have brought to this project is very little. Mostly, I have been around Nebraska football a long time and tried to pay attention. The players, coaches, and support personnel who have fed a state's passion and helped to create its identity have done the work. I have only observed it. So, first and foremost, my thanks go to them, from the All-American who answers repeated questions without complaint to the fifth-string, senior walk-on who never played a down when it mattered, and to everyone in between.

Thanks to all those with whom I have worked over the years and continue to work, those who have treated me as if I knew something when, in fact, they were mostly being nice. And thanks to those newspaper reporters of long ago, including Cy Sherman, Walt Dobbins, Frederick Ware, Gregg McBride, and Wally Provost, who helped preserve some of the stories recounted here.

Thanks to *Huskers Illustrated* editor Brian Hill, not only for help in selecting photos but also for allowing me to continue to write for the magazine as a freelancer, and to Lois Brinton at the university's photo services, for providing priceless pictures from the earliest days of Cornhusker football.

Thanks to Nebraska sports information director Chris Anderson, who turned the Globe Pequot Press my way, football SID Keith Mann, and the rest of the sports information staff, football and otherwise. Also, thanks to the folks at the Globe Pequot Press, among them Mike Urban and Juliana

Gribbins, whose job it was to make sure what was written was grammatically sound and semantically clear.

Thanks to all of these people and many more who have helped along the way.

What's in a Name?

The first time Trev Alberts met Tom Osborne was when the Nebraska coach came to Cedar Falls, Iowa. Nebraska assistant John Melton had handled the recruiting to that point. But Trev's dad wondered how interested the Cornhuskers were and asked Melton why Osborne hadn't visited his son. "If he really thought this highly of Trev, wouldn't he make a trip here?" Ken Alberts asked.

Soon after, Osborne flew to Cedar Falls to visit the Alberts family. Before they went out to eat, "my mom was lining us up for pictures," Trev recalled with a smile, several years later. It was a major event. And when the photos came back, his mom remarked, "Coach is bigger than you, Trev."

Trev's dad made dinner reservations at the Broom Factory, as the name indicates, a restaurant in a former broom factory, located on the Cedar River, as well as the "nicest restaurant in town," according to Trev. Mr. Alberts also made certain that the table at which they ate had a red tablecloth, in honor of Osborne. Theirs was the only red tablecloth in the restaurant, a fact that the Cornhusker coach acknowledged.

Osborne came across as "very laid back, down to earth," in marked contrast to Iowa Coach Hayden Fry, who wore snakeskin boots and a large gold wristwatch. His family is "pretty conservative, Midwestern Iowa," said Alberts, and "my mom was put off immediately by what she perceived as [Fry's] arrogance. But boy, she really took to Tom Osborne. She thought that guy was all right."

Trev's family also is strong in its religious faith, as is Osborne. When asked about that, Osborne said he didn't have time to share all of his beliefs but that he would leave a copy of his first book, *More Than Winning*, for them to read, that it would provide insight into his religious beliefs. However, the book would have to be returned, Osborne told them, otherwise it would be a violation of NCAA rules.

Despite Osborne's visit to Cedar Falls, Alberts never imagined he would go to Nebraska. He had grown up in Iowa, with the understanding that if he ever had the opportunity to play college athletics, he would do so for his home state's university. His parents were Hawkeye fans and he had made an oral commitment to Iowa early on. Just talking to Nebraska was "kind of like a slap in the face," he said.

But after Osborne's visit, Trev wanted to take a trip to Lincoln, just to look around. And his dad sensed that. So he and his parents piled into the family Cadillac, which had belonged to his grandfather, and drove to Lincoln, with the understanding that after he was wined and dined by Nebraska, he would still follow through on the commitment to accept a football scholarship from Iowa.

It didn't turn out that way, of course. During the ride home the subject of whether he still wanted to go to Iowa didn't come up until they reached Des Moines. His parents understood, as only parents can. "I think it was kind of hitting them that their son might be leaving, going to Nebraska," Alberts said. Finally, his dad broke the silence, saying they really wanted him at Iowa, but they would understand if he went to Nebraska. In fact, after visiting, they would almost encourage him to do so. "It was like a ton of bricks taken off my shoulders," Trev recalled. "That's what I was waiting for." He told his parents he was going to Nebraska. The next day,

Nebraska went to a 4–3 base defense to utilize the skills of players such as Trev Alberts, the Butkus Award winner in 1993. (Courtesy Huskers Illustrated)

Hawkeye assistant Dan McCarney called to check on how the visit had gone and got the bad news.

Alberts didn't remember much about his trip to Nebraska. He met with deans and professors, as well as with players and coaches, and toured the facilities, all standard recruiting visit procedure. But he hasn't forgotten the billboards and the signs coming into Lincoln, "Big Red" this and "Husker" that, nor pulling off of Interstate 80 and onto Cornhusker Highway. "Man, Cornhusker Highway," he said.

Cornhusker Highway didn't get its name from the university's athletic teams, not directly anyway. But the roots of "Cornhusker" run deep into the past, back to 1900, generally regarded as the year Nebraska's teams became the Cornhuskers, through the efforts of a Lincoln sportswriter, Charles Sumner "Cy" Sherman, and a university journalism professor, Albert Watkins Jr.

Prior to 1900 Nebraska's football team, which first played in 1890, was known by various nicknames, among them the unimaginative Nebraskans, Old Gold Knights—the school colors didn't officially become scarlet and cream until 1902, according to Robert Manley's *Centennial History of the University of Nebraska*—Rattlesnake Boys, Tree-planters, Antelopes, and Bugeaters.

The name Bugeaters came from "the insect-devouring bull bats that were common on the prairies," according to the *Omaha World-Herald's* Frederick Ware and Gregg McBride in *50 Years of Football*, published in 1940. The name had more to it than that, however. In a story about a drought in Nebraska in the 1870s, an Eastern newspaper reporter wrote that since bugs devoured the crops, all that was left for Nebraskans to eat were bugs. The reference might not have been complimentary in its intent, but it reflected the hearty nature of those who had struggled and survived the drought.

A young Cy Sherman and his father, the first publisher of the *Plattsmouth Tribune*, were among those who attended the Nebraska–Iowa football game at Omaha during a blizzard on Thanksgiving Day of 1893. Apparently he considered Bugeaters to be an inappropriate nickname for the Nebraska team, which won 20–18, and after becoming a sportswriter two years later, he set about changing it.

After Nebraska defeated Iowa 36–0 at Omaha a year later, the university newspaper, the *Hesperian Student*, proclaimed, "We have met the 'cornhuskers' and they are ours." Though the term *cornhuskers* might have been applied somewhat derisively, Sherman must have considered it otherwise because by 1899 he was referring to Nebraska's football team as the Cornhuskers. Additionally, Professor Watkins led a movement on campus to adopt the nickname. By and by it was Sherman who became known as the "father of the Cornhuskers." In 1933 the university's "N" club made him an honorary member, presenting him with a gold football and varsity letter.

In 1907 the student yearbook changed its name from "Sombrero" to "Cornhusker," and in 1946 the legislature made Nebraska the "Cornhusker State." Sherman was presented the pen with which Governor Dwight Griswold signed the bill that made the now-familiar nickname official.

Sherman also became known as the "dean of American sportswriters" during a career of nearly sixty years, according to the *Lincoln Star*. He spent thirty-one of those years writing about the Cornhuskers as sports editor of the *Star*. But describing him as the dean of sportswriters was more than just self-serving by the *Star*. Sherman was nationally respected and responsible for helping to establish the Associated Press football rankings in 1936.

Through his efforts the AP began releasing a weekly top ten, compiled through voting by its members. Originally, only newspapers were involved, one vote each, which could be cast or not. A dozen years after the poll's inception, 150 to 250 votes were being received by each week's Monday deadline, "depending upon the shock that Saturday's results have produced," the AP reported.

Prior to 1936 Alan Gould, the general sports editor for the wire service, picked a top ten, according to the AP. But when college football "moved beyond the bounds of the Yale–Harvard–Princeton triumvirate," there was a call for change. As early as 1915, Sherman had argued that Nebraska had produced the best football team in the land. The Cornhuskers were 8–0 and had scored more points than any other team in the country except Rutgers and Vanderbilt, both of which had lost.

Nebraska's success was such that it was extended an invitation in December to play in the Rose Bowl game. But the university Athletic Board declined. The Cornhusker coach considered scheduling a postseason game against an Eastern power, such as Syracuse or Brown. But soon after a 52–7 Homecoming victory against Iowa at Nebraska Field, he accepted a job at Indiana. The coach was E. O. "Jumbo" Stiehm.

Football had emerged as the major sport at Nebraska in 1900, Guy E. Reed wrote in the *Semi-Centennial Anniversary Book*, published in 1919. Reed was a track letterman at Nebraska, a sprinter, qualifying for the Olympic Trials at Evanston, Illinois, in 1912, who later worked in the athletic department. Nebraska posted a 6–1–1 record in 1900, under first-year coach Walter C. "Bummy" Booth, a Princeton graduate. But it wasn't until Stiehm's five-year tenure as coach that football came of age at the university. "Cornhusker football today is fundamentally the football of the Stiehm Roller era," Ware wrote a quarter of a century later. Although Stiehm's departure was unexpected and controversial, "the public's interest was to continue growing, and the college football ambitions of Nebraska high school boys were to be permanently centered on a block 'N' of scarlet and cream," according to Ware.

Nebraska had enjoyed success before Stiehm's arrival. Booth's teams were a combined 46–8–1 over six seasons, and during his tenure, Nebraska had a twenty-four-game winning streak from 1901 to 1904. His 1902 team didn't allow a point in nine games, while scoring 159. The Cornhuskers also defeated Lincoln High School, from which many of Nebraska's players came, in an exhibition game to open the season, 27–0. Even so, Booth had his detractors and resigned for a more lucrative law practice in New York City. Amos Foster succeeded him for one 6–4 season, then left for a law practice in Cincinnati, Ohio, leaving the job open to W. C. "King" Cole, who was coaching at Virginia, after playing for Fielding Yost at Michigan.

Cole's final team in 1910 won seven of eight games and Nebraska's first outright conference championship. The Cornhuskers shut out their final five opponents, defeating Haskell 119–0 at Lincoln in Cole's last game as coach. The Missouri Valley Conference had passed a rule requiring member institutions to hire a full-time coach. And the job didn't pay enough for Cole. But it did for a youthful Stiehm, who had been a multisport athlete at Wisconsin and had competed against Nebraska in basketball, in fact. He coached the high school team in Fort Atkinson, Wisconsin, while still a university student. He also taught history. Most recently, he had been the athletic director and coach at Ripon College. Ripon tried to keep him but couldn't match Nebraska's salary offer.

Stiehm earned the nickname "Jumbo" not because of his height, 6'4", but rather because of his large feet. University students didn't refer to him by the nickname, and apparently, they didn't trifle with him in other ways either. After the sports editor of the student newspaper observed that the Cornhuskers would "go" because they had "so much Stiehm" behind them, the student yearbook later reported, Stiehm went to the newspaper's office and "devastated the sporting editor, so that he resigned."

Stiehm's distaste for wordplay on his name and reference to his nickname weren't all that drew his ire. After officials ruled that an apparent Owen Frank touchdown didn't count in a 6–6 tie with Michigan to finish Stiehm's first season as Nebraska's coach, the yearbook claimed that he went home, "took down all the pretty girl pictures in his room and put them in a Bible, stuffed a handkerchief in the telephone transmitter, took off his collar, and said several little things in a whisper that were so hot they peppered the 'Ump's' soup next morning." Even so, Stiehm was "modest and retiring," the anonymous author wrote.

His players were, for the most part, undersized, averaging less than 180 pounds per man. But they made up for it with discipline and tenacity. Stiehm was the "John McGraw of the gridiron," *Lincoln Journal* sports editor Walt Dobbins wrote, referring to the New York Giants Baseball Hall of Fame manager. They "had to obey without question

The Stiehmrollers' Finest Season

Coach "Jumbo" Stiehm's finest season was probably his last at Nebraska in 1915, when his Stiehmrollers outscored their eight opponents by a combined 282–39. Stiehm was so confident of a victory against Nebraska Wesleyan that he and Dick Rutherford, his team captain, skipped that game to scout the next week's Missouri Valley Conference opponent, Kansas.

Drake 48–13
Kansas State 31–0
Washburn 47–0
Notre Dame 20–19
at Iowa State 21–0
Nebraska Wesleyan 30–0
at Kansas 33–0
Iowa 52–7

orders that often were a dictator's iron command," wrote Ware. Stiehm's Cornhuskers were "quarrelsome, challenging, fiercely loyal" and relentless. They played through injuries, even broken bones. And they lost only twice in five seasons under Stiehm's direction.

His record as football coach—he also coached basketball—was 35-2-3, with one of the losses and two of the ties coming in his first season, 1911. His Cornhuskers won five consecutive Missouri Valley Conference championships. After a 13–0 loss at Minnesota in mid-October of 1912, his teams wouldn't lose again. A week later, the Cornhuskers defeated Adrian College 41–0, beginning a school-record thirty-four-game unbeaten streak that would continue into the first of E. J. "Doc" Stewart's two seasons as coach.

During the Stiehm era the Nebraska football team was referred to as "Stiehmrollers" as often as Cornhuskers, according to Ware. And when they defeated perennial power Minnesota 7–0 at Lincoln in 1913—only their second victory in an annual series dating to 1900—Gophers coach Henry Williams terminated the series. Stiehm had used photographs of Williams's vaunted "shift" to devise a defense to stop it. Frank, who had finished playing and become an assistant, took the photos during the previous year's game.

Two years later, Notre Dame replaced Minnesota on Nebraska's schedule, and some scouting by Knute Rockne, an assistant to Coach Jesse Harper, went awry. Rockne thought he had detected something that gave away what the Cornhuskers' Guy Chamberlin intended to do. But Chamberlin crossed up Notre Dame, scoring two touchdowns in the 20–19 victory at Lincoln, witnessed by a reported 8,000. Chamberlin, the "Champ," came from Blue Springs, Nebraska, by way of Nebraska Wesleyan, where he played two seasons before being persuaded to transfer. After spending his first season on the Cornhuskers' freshman team as a result of his transfer, he led Nebraska to a 15–0–1 record in 1914 and 1915. He played end as well as in the backfield and scored a remarkable sixteen touchdowns in his final season.

Walter Eckersall, who officiated the Cornhuskers' final game in 1915, wrote afterward in a Chicago newspaper, "The scarlet men of the plains, the men of Jumbo Stiehm are an astonishing team. I am sure the Missouri Valley region has never seen the equal of this year's Nebraska

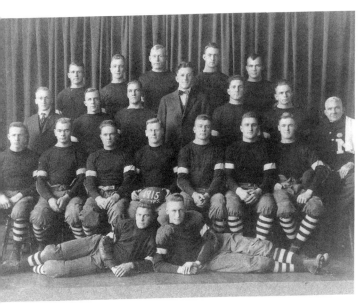

The "Stiehmrollers" were 8–0 in Coach Jumbo Stiehm's final season, 1915. The 6'4" Stiehm is standing in the middle (coat and bow tie). On the far right, towel on his shoulder, is longtime trainer Jack Best. To Best's immediate right, seated, is Guy Chamberlin, Nebraska's second All-American. (Courtesy UNL Photography)

eleven." Chamberlin earned All-America recognition, a year after Vic Halligan was the first Cornhusker to be so honored.

According to various sources, Nebraska's athletic department revenue was as much as $35,000 in 1915. Though the Cornhuskers were turned down for membership in the Western Conference (now the Big Ten), as they had been in 1900, they were beginning to draw national attention. There was talk of replacing Nebraska Field, built in 1907, with a larger concrete and steel structure.

Men in Black

Nebraska's Blackshirt tradition began in the mid-1960s, when NCAA substitution rules were amended to allow two-platoon football. Coach Bob Devaney used contrasting pullovers to differentiate offensive players from defensive players during practice. Assistant Mike Corgan, who was noted for his frugality, was sent to a local sporting goods store to purchase the pullovers and returned with black ones. The store-owner had given him a good deal because the black ones hadn't sold particularly well.

The sleeveless black shirts were handed out to first-team defensive players each day before practice and collected afterward to be washed. So a player might have a black pullover one day and not the next, depending on how well he had practiced. "There probably wasn't a day when we didn't make switches," George Kelly recalled years later. Kelly was Devaney's defensive line coach until 1968.

By 1969, when Monte Kiffin had succeeded Kelly as defensive line coach and was coordinating the defense, the term *Blackshirt* had become synonymous with the Cornhuskers. The tradition grew, including the distribution of black jerseys with the players' numbers on them replacing the pullovers, and during Charlie McBride's tenure as defensive coordinator and line coach (1977–99), it enjoyed a national reputation. "People around the country know," he said.

"It's hard to put into words the significance of a Blackshirt, the amount of pride it brings," said Kyle Vanden Bosch, a rush end and captain in 2000. "A Blackshirt is a symbol. It's something

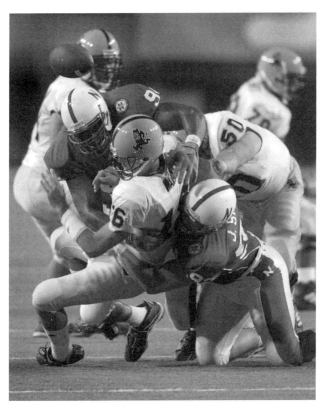

Nebraska's Blackshirts force a fumble. (Courtesy Huskers Illustrated*)*

you've just got to live up to," Chris Kelsay, also a rush end and captain in 2002, said. "It's something that makes you relentless, makes you drive all day out there at practice, all year on the field and all year off the field, because it's more than just the team at hand. It's for all the Blackshirts that have ever played."

Some have suggested that the "Blackshirts" were Nebraska's version of Louisiana State's famed "Chinese Bandits" defense. Kelly, however, dismissed that. "I wasn't very well read on Southern football," he said. "Honestly, it was an accident of availability."

The enthusiasm was dashed, however, when Stiehm accepted the job as athletic director and coach at Indiana. Money was the sticking point; Indiana offered more than Nebraska was willing to pay. Stiehm's annual salary, which had begun at $2,000, was $3,500. And he would have stayed for a raise to $4,250, he said, even though Indiana offered more—later reported to be $4,500. But university professors were upset that a coach would earn more than they did, and rumors that local businessmen would make up any difference in what the university was willing to pay proved not to be true.

Given that football generated most of the $35,000 in revenue, Stiehm was convinced that the university could meet his request without help from businessmen. In any case he said he would remain at Nebraska through the end of the basketball season, after the Athletic Board released him from a "gentleman's agreement" that would have kept him until September 1917. Stiehm emphasized that he had not broken the terms of a written contract. But what began as an amicable separation quickly deteriorated after Stiehm hired Dick Rutherford, the Cornhusker captain in 1915, to go with him to Indiana as an assistant coach.

Rutherford, who came from Beatrice, Nebraska, was "rated by many as the greatest all 'round athlete the university ever turned out," the *Nebraska State Journal* reported. In addition to clearing the way for Chamberlin with his aggressive blocks out of the backfield, Rutherford was a "wrestling champion, gymnast and swimmer." He also competed on the basketball and track teams. He had the support of the student body as Stiehm's replacement, according to the newspaper. "More feeling has been stirred up over the Rutherford deal than over anything that has occurred in the athletic department in years."

Indiana released Rutherford from his commitment with Stiehm's blessing, and he was hired as a Nebraska assistant at $2,500 annually, $700 more than Indiana would have paid and an unheard of salary for an assistant. Stiehm resigned immediately. According to a *Nebraska State Journal* story in early January 1916, following the announcement that he wouldn't remain until spring, "by most followers of the sport, Stiehm was regarded as the greatest coach Nebraska ever had." His success wouldn't continue at Indiana, where his football teams were a combined 20–18–1 from 1916 to 1921. He died of cancer in 1922 at age thirty-five.

Ninety years after Sherman gave Nebraska its nickname, Alberts was impressed that his trip to the university included a drive along Cornhusker Highway. Though he hadn't grown up in the state, he embraced the tradition. "In my heart, I felt Nebraska was the right place for me," he said.

He was right for Nebraska as well. He was a 6'4", 240-pound outside linebacker, strong and swift, with a quick first step, and because of his skills, the Cornhuskers changed their base defense from a "50" front to an attacking 4–3, to take advantage of his pass-rushing skills. The change in defensive philosophy was a significant factor in Nebraska's winning three national championships in Osborne's final four seasons, even though Alberts completed his eligibility one season before that run began.

Such changes "always evolve with the personnel you have and what's happening in football," said Osborne. "It was just more that we fell into it, not a stroke of genius." Alberts was a consensus All-American as a senior in 1993 and the Cornhuskers' first Butkus Award winner, as well as the *Football News* "Defensive Player of the Year." He started the season strong. "He's probably had more impact through five games than anybody we've ever had at that position," Osborne said prior to the conference opener at Oklahoma State. And he never let up, setting a school record with fifteen sacks.

Despite suffering a dislocated right elbow in the final regular-season game against Oklahoma, he returned for the Cornhuskers' near-upset of Florida State in the Orange Bowl game and sacked Heisman Trophy winner Charlie Ward three times. Without a doubt, he could have played for Stiehm.

Competing in Silence

oach Tom Osborne described Kenny Walker as "possibly the best pass rusher in the country" during his Cornhusker career. He earned letters in 1989 and 1990, when he was a first-team all-conference selection. At 6'4" and 240 pounds, he was undersized for a defensive tackle. And he was deaf, having contracted spinal meningitis when he was two years old. But he was so athletically talented, "he's going to be illegal," defensive coordinator Charlie McBride predicted when he arrived from Crane, Texas.

Nebraska assistants George Darlington and Tony Samuel learned sign language to better communicate with Walker, who was accompanied to class by an interpreter paid through the Handicapped Services Office of Nebraska's Educational Center for Disabled Students. He earned a bachelor's degree in art.

If You Build It, They Will Come

In mid-November of 2003, Nebraska Athletic Director Steve Pederson announced plans for an expansion project that would include a new football locker room and indoor practice facility and allow for the relocation of the training room, weight room, and administrative offices, all at the north end of Memorial Stadium. The project also would add 5,000 seats to the North Stadium.

The cost of the project was estimated at nearly $50 million, with the additional seats providing the revenue to cover the cost of their construction, an estimated $9 million. The Tom and Nancy Osborne Athletic Complex would absorb Schulte Field House, retaining some elements of the venerable structure, which was completed in 1946. "It will be the finest facility in college football and will impact our program for decades to come," said Pederson. The new facility will be a far cry from the way things were in 1922.

Nebraska Field

Jack Best, his legs all but useless from the ravages of age, was bundled in blankets and carried from his office in the basement of Grant Hall to a taxi, which took him to nearby Nebraska Field. Then two Cornhusker football players

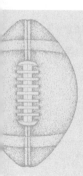

No Place like Home

Although Memorial Stadium was dedicated with a scoreless tie, Nebraska has fared well there. Through the 2003 season, the Cornhuskers' all-time record at the stadium was 343-102-13 (a .763 winning percentage).

lifted him out of the taxi and carried him to the locker room, where he addressed the team. Best told the players he would be watching them for the last time when they played Notre Dame that afternoon, Thanksgiving Day 1922. And he wanted them to win the game. When Best finished speaking, Coach Fred Dawson began a low chant of his name. "Tears streamed down the cheeks of the giants who pounded onto the field a few minutes later," *Omaha World-Herald* sports editor Frederick Ware wrote several years later, recounting what he had been told in a letter from Burke Taylor, a Nebraska alum and witness to the pregame proceedings.

Only a tie with Army blemished the record of Coach Knute Rockne's Notre Dame team, which included the players whom Grantland Rice would later immortalize as the "Four Horsemen" (Jim Crowley, Don Miller, Elmer Layden, and Harry Stuhldreher). Coach Fred Dawson's Cornhuskers were equally formidable. They were Missouri Valley Conference champions for a second consecutive season and had lost just once, at Syracuse earlier that month.

Interest in the game, as was always the case when Notre Dame came to Lincoln, was such that Nebraska Field's wooden stands were filled to overflowing. People climbed trees to watch or perched atop a nearby power plant's coal pile to get a view of the game. Some were turned away because the tickets they had purchased from scalpers were counterfeit. Because of concern that those who couldn't see might storm the gates, the university arranged for a crude play-by-play shouted by megaphone from windows of nearby newspaper offices. Some 15,000 paid their way in, with another 1,000 or so freeloading.

The crowd acknowledged Best's presence, according to the student yearbook, which noted that few "will forget the smile on Jack's face as thousands of Cornhuskers rose and paid him tribute." Best had been in failing health. "His hair grew white and his body gnarled in the service of the university," the yearbook noted. "But his brown eyes twinkled and his voice was merry to the last day that he sat in his old chair down in the varsity room," the one in the basement of the armory.

Two years before, in December, a reception in honor of Best's seventy-fifth birthday had been held in that room. The occasion had merited local newspaper coverage equal to and alongside a story on the death of Notre Dame All-American George Gipp, as a result of complications from pneumonia at age twenty-five.

Best was beloved by the students. He arrived at the university in 1888, beginning as a night watchman and then serving as an athletic trainer. "No history of Nebraska would be half complete without some tribute to the service of our beloved trainer," Guy E. Reed wrote in a fifty-year history of Nebraska athletics, published in 1922. When the first football team was organized in 1890, Best also helped coach. "He knows the tricks of the game as featured by high hurdling and the block formation plays and he knows the tricks and plays of the present scientific contest," wrote Reed.

Best was born in England and had done some boxing, under the name "Jimmie Grimes," before his son convinced him to move to the United States and resume the tanning trade, which is how he had made a living in London. He moved to Lincoln to utilize his experience as a boxing trainer. He was known affectionately by university students as "Jimmy" and accorded mystical healing powers. He could make aches and pains disappear "almost by no more than touching the spot," the yearbook claimed. When his health began to fail, the lettermen's club raised money to send him on a curative western vacation. He remained at Nebraska despite opportunities to go elsewhere. "There isn't anything I wouldn't do for the boys. I feel just like they are mine," he once said.

Best had seen Nebraska Field being built in 1908 on land secured by the Athletic Board for that purpose, just to the south of where Memorial Stadium is located now. The playing field ran east and west and was a far cry from the first field on which the university's football teams played, near the engineering building. Players had to walk that field beforehand to remove rocks and other debris. And it wasn't much more accommodating for spectators, with only a few wooden-plank seats and limited room to stand. As a result early football teams would often play at a municipal base-ball park or, on occasion, in Omaha.

The first game at Nebraska Field was played on October 23, 1909 — after two off-campus games in Lincoln and another in Omaha. The Cornhuskers of Coach W. C.

Good Sports

After Florida State defeated Nebraska 18–14 at Memorial Stadium in 1980, Seminoles Coach Bobby Bowden said the victory might have been the biggest in school history. Nebraska was number three in the Associated Press poll at the time, following a victory at Penn State the previous week.

Despite the frustration of the loss, made worse by the fact the Cornhuskers couldn't hold a 14–3 halftime lead and lost a fumble at the Florida State 3 yard line with twelve seconds remaining, Nebraska fans were respectful of the visitors from Tallahassee, prompting Bowden to write an open letter to them. The letter, published in the Lincoln and Omaha newspapers the next week, said in part: "I actually had the feeling that when we upset the Nebraska team, that instead of hate and spite the Nebraska fans thanked us for coming to Lincoln and putting on a good show. This is nearly unheard of in today's society." Bowden brought Florida State to Lincoln three more times in the next six seasons and the Seminoles received similar treatment, even after winning again in 1985, 17–13.

Nebraska fans still have a reputation for hospitality, though not to the same degree.

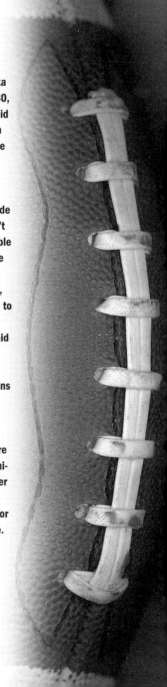

"King" Cole played Iowa to a 6–6 standoff. Cole's final team in 1910 would play six games there, winning them all, the last by 119–0 against Haskell Institute, payback for a 16–5 loss against Haskell the previous year at Lawrence, Kansas.

A key factor in the building of Nebraska Field had been Nebraska's membership in the Missouri Valley Conference, which also required full-time football coaches. Cole, who was earning nearly $3,000 a year as a part-time coach, didn't want the job full-time, so the Athletic Board took applications from those who did. As many as fifty candidates applied, including former players Johnny Bender and Maurice Benedict, both of whom enjoyed student support. But the Board hired E. O. "Jumbo" Stiehm.

The success under Stiehm was such, the *Lincoln Star* reported, that football revenue was an impressive $35,000 in 1915, his final season at Nebraska, and there was talk of replacing Nebraska Field with a concrete and steel stadium to accommodate growing interest in the Cornhusker football teams. But that wouldn't become reality for another eight years and four more coaches.

The Notre Dame game in 1922 was the last to be played at Nebraska Field. The campaign to raise more than $400,000 for the construction of what would be Memorial Stadium had begun a month earlier. The Cornhuskers, encouraged by Best's pregame words, said good-bye to Nebraska Field with a 14–6 victory. As it turned out, they also had said their good-byes to "Jimmy." Less than two months later, he died at age seventy-seven. "Thousands of students and alumni" attended Best's funeral, according to the student yearbook, which might have overstated the number but certainly not the sentiment. "Long and faith-

Coach Jumbo Stiehm's 1912 team went 7–1 to win the Missouri Valley Conference championship. (Courtesy UNL Photography)

fully Jack served us; long and tenderly will we cherish his memory," read the dedication.

Memorial Stadium

Nebraska was first-and-goal at the Kansas 7 yard line in the third quarter, poised to break a scoreless tie. Verne Lewellen gained 1 yard on first down, and Dave Noble gained a combined 5 yards on second and third, leaving the ball 1 yard away. Herb Dewitz got the call on fourth down. The senior halfback from Stanton, Nebraska, tried for the final yard off left tackle and appeared to have it before being pushed back by the Kansas defense. "The Nebraska sections were in a frenzy," according to a Lincoln newspaper account. The stands went "wild, thinking Herb Dewitz had crossed." The players were pulled from the pile, however, and the referee spotted the ball inches from the end zone. He was adamant about the spot. The visiting Jayhawks had held for a second time—just before halftime, Noble had picked up 3 yards on a fourth-and-4 at the Kansas 7 yard line.

Nebraska would have no better opportunities for getting on the scoreboard and the closest Kansas would come was late in the game, when it reached the Cornhusker 6 yard line only to fall a yard short on fourth down. So the game ended as it had begun, 0–0. That was particularly frustrating for Nebraska, which not only was celebrating Homecoming but also dedicating a new stadium.

The date was October 20, 1923. And work on the stadium wasn't complete. But the dedication went on as planned, with special trains offering reduced fares to bring fans to Lincoln from Omaha and Lawrence, Kansas. Early in the week, John Selleck, the business manager for the athletic department, dismissed rumors that all of the tickets for the game had been sold. Nearly 5,000 remained, he announced. The day's festivities included a downtown parade organized by the university ROTC in the morning and a dedication speech delivered by Charles C. Richards, the president of Lehigh University and a former dean of Nebraska's College of Agriculture. Then an estimated 20,000 watched the score-less tie, a "moral victory for the invading Jayhawkers," the *Lincoln Journal's* John Bentley wrote.

The Kansas defense had shut out its first three opponents and would shut out two of the remaining four, allowing only two field goals all season. So there was no disgrace in that, really. But the Cornhuskers had fallen victim to "that spectre known as a stadium jinx," wrote Bentley. The year before, Nebraska had defeated the Jayhawks 28–0 on the day they dedicated their new stadium, and the game at which their Homecoming was celebrated. The same fate had befallen Ohio State in 1922, when the Buckeyes dedicated Ohio Stadium with a 19–0 loss against archrival Michigan. Nebraska's Memorial Stadium was patterned after Ohio Stadium, in structure but not in capacity, though the need for more seating was a significant factor in its creation. There had been talk of replacing the wooden stands of Nebraska Field when Stiehm was coach, but the impetus came with a "reawakening of the Nebraska spirit" under Fred Dawson, the student newspaper reported.

Dawson, a Princeton graduate, arrived in 1921 and coached the Cornhuskers to a 7–1 season, which included a 10–0 victory at perennial power and Nebraska nemesis Pittsburgh as well as a Missouri Valley Conference championship. The Cornhuskers would celebrate another conference title and 7–1 record in 1922, with the fund-raising drive for a new stadium well under way by season's end.

The stadium was located just to the north of where Nebraska Field had been, but running north and south, and surrounded by a quarter-mile track, with the projected main entrance at the south end. The main entrance, however, would be located on the stadium's east side, where the façade still provides evidence of Nebraska's membership in the Missouri Valley Conference when the stadium was constructed. The seals of eight other schools also are embedded in the concrete. In addition to those of longtime conference rivals Iowa State, Kansas, Kansas State, Missouri, and Oklahoma, those of Drake, Grinnell, and Washington University of St. Louis, Missouri, have been preserved there. The stadium was to be "a permanent memorial to those Nebraskans who made the supreme sacrifice in France" in World War I, the student yearbook reported. And its projected seating capacity, when complete, was to be between 25,000 and 40,000, or about twice that of Nebraska Field.

Students pledged $100,000 of the cost of construction, the student newspaper reported, and the groundbreaking took place on April 23, 1923, when Chancellor Samuel Avery "plowed a furrow" through a large letter N formed by members of the lettermen's club and the women's athletic association. The cornerstone was laid during the university's annual spring roundup and the bid was let on May 2. Parsons Construction Company of Omaha had eighty-nine working days to complete the project, with thirty-one of those days lost all or in part because of weather problems. The grading required forty men, fifty horses, and two caterpillar tractors. A giant shovel moved 700 cubic yards of earth a day. The stadium included 16,000 cubic yards of concrete, 350,000 feet of lumber, and 600 tons of steel reinforcement.

It was far from complete for the first game, played on October 13. A generously estimated 15,000, which included youngsters who were admitted free, watched the Cornhuskers defeat Oklahoma 24–0. A month later, after the dedication game tie, temporary bleachers had to be located at the ends of the field to accommodate a crowd estimated at 30,000 to watch—who else?—Notre Dame. "Again, had Nebraska not been on the schedule, the season would have been without defeat," *Omaha World-Herald* sports editor

Memorial Stadium groundbreaking, spring 1923. (Courtesy UNL Photography)

Frederick Ware wrote of Rockne's team. Noble scored touchdowns on a 24-yard run and an 18-yard pass from Rufus DeWitz in a 14–6 Cornhusker victory.

The Streak

At 2:00 P.M. on November 3, 1962, a sellout crowd of 36,501 settled in at Memorial Stadium to watch Nebraska play Missouri. The game was a focus of Homecoming weekend, which contributed to all of the tickets being sold. In addition the Cornhuskers were undefeated, at 6–0, and "sensationally improved" under new coach Bob Devaney, *Lincoln Star* sports editor Don Bryant wrote.

Nebraska had not enjoyed a winning season since 1954, and enthusiasm was growing victory by victory. Nevertheless, Missouri also was a factor in the size of the crowd. Two weeks before, tickets had remained for a 26–6 victory against ever hapless Kansas State. And the season opener against overmatched South Dakota, Devaney's debut as head coach, had drawn just 26,953.

In contrast Nebraska and Missouri were longtime rivals, and the only blemish on the Tigers' record was a tie at Minnesota, which had been nationally ranked at the time. Plus, they had won the previous five games in the Nebraska series, including the last two in Lincoln by a combined 59–0. The game had Orange Bowl implications—though Oklahoma would end up in Miami on New Year's Day—and the potential to become an offensive show. Nebraska ranked fourth nationally in total offense and fifth in scoring, while Missouri ranked third nationally in rushing offense. The matchup was attractive enough that CBS television carried it regionally, with famed announcer Mel Allen handling play-by-play.

There were interesting subplots as well. Devaney and Missouri coach Dan Devine had been assistants together on the Michigan State staff of the legendary Duffy Daugherty, and Devaney also had interviewed for the job at Missouri when Devine was hired to replace Frank Broyles in 1958.

The crowd was the second largest of the season at Memorial Stadium. North Carolina State had attracted 36,867, the largest crowd to see a game in Lincoln since the second game of the 1960 season, when 39,363 crammed in to watch a Nebraska team ranked number twelve nationally in the Associated Press poll, a week after opening with a

Clean Shaven

Nebraska's first loss under Coach Bob Devaney in 1962 was also the first sellout at Memorial Stadium in a continuing NCAA-record streak. Missouri defeated the Cornhuskers 16–7 in Nebraska's Homecoming game. The loss was the Cornhuskers' sixth in a row against Missouri, prompting Bob Brown, a junior lineman to vow he would grow a goatee and not shave until Nebraska finally won against the Tigers. A year later at Columbia, Missouri, it did, 13–12, and Brown's goatee came off. Paul Schneider and George Sullivan, the Cornhusker trainers, applied the shaving cream, and Brown's teammate Tony Jeter, an All-America end, applied the razor.

Brown, who would earn consensus All-America honors that season as an offensive guard and linebacker, was the best two-way player he ever coached, Devaney said.

14–13 upset of fourth-ranked Texas at Austin, lose to Minnesota.

In any case, the night before the Missouri game, what Lincoln newspapers described as "fun lovers" broke into the stadium and shuffled cards to be used for the halftime show, rearranging them "to form pictures other than those planned," and providing an omen of what was to come. The Cornhuskers lost three fumbles and had three passes intercepted, and they would have been shut out if not for an 88-yard interception return for a touchdown by Noel Martin in the second quarter. Missouri converted three of the turnovers into scores in a 16–7 victory.

Interest in the Cornhuskers didn't diminish, however. A crowd of 34,329 filled Memorial Stadium to watch a

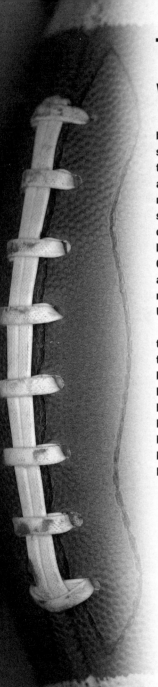

Touch of Luck

When the varsity locker room was moved from the north field house to the South Stadium before the opener against UCLA in 1973, several players went to Coach Tom Osborne to remind him that the horseshoe hanging above the door of the old locker room needed to be moved as well. The horseshoe had been there as long as anyone could remember, and players touched it for luck on their way to the field. Though Osborne said he wasn't superstitious, he agreed that the horseshoe should be moved, if for no other reason than so UCLA wouldn't have it to touch.

Cocaptains Daryl White, an offensive tackle, and John Dutton, a defensive tackle, lifted Bob Thornton, a defensive back, so he could reach up and put the horseshoe in place above the double doors leading to the tunnel adjacent to the locker room. The horseshoe is still there to be touched for luck and will undoubtedly be moved back to the north end when Nebraska's new locker room is built.

14–0 victory against Oklahoma State two weeks later, increasing Nebraska's home sellout streak to two. Entering 2004 the streak had swelled to an NCAA-record 262, with no end in sight.

Memorial Stadium's official capacity was 31,080 in 1962, when William Henry Harrison "Tippy" Dye became Nebraska athletic director. Three weeks before officially beginning his duties, Dye announced three goals: to hire the best football coach available, to make Nebraska a national championship contender, and to enlarge the stadium. "We are hoping to get our stadium to a place where it will seat more people, so we'll be able to schedule better teams," he told the Lincoln newspapers.

Dye achieved each of those goals, although Devaney had succeeded him as athletic director when the Cornhuskers won their first national championships in 1970 and 1971. But they had made a run at a national title in 1965 and again in 1966 under Devaney, the Hall of Fame coach whom Dye hired. And Memorial Stadium had begun to grow almost immediately under Dye's direction. In 1964 the south end zone section was built, creating a horseshoe and increasing the official capacity to 44,829. In 1965 the center of the north end zone section was completed, increasing the capacity to 50,807. And in 1966 the north end zone section was expanded, increasing capacity to 62,644. The final major expansion occurred in 1972, when the south end zone section was extended, adding some 11,000 seats to bring the official count to 73,650. The capacity was reduced slightly with remodeling in 1994, increased with the addition of skyboxes in 1999, and then reduced slightly again in 2000. Even so, crowds of more than 78,000 have filled Memorial Stadium since then, with

Western side of Memorial Stadium after an improvement project was completed in 1999. (Courtesy Huskers Illustrated)

a record 78,268 on hand for the Texas game in 2002—the Cornhuskers lost 27–24.

The official capacity through the 2003 season was 73,918. By 2005 it is projected to be nearly 80,000, or more than twice the number of those who watched the first game in the streak against Missouri more than forty years ago. The Tigers have won only four times in Lincoln since then.

Trainwreck and Mr. Touchdown

For the most part Nebraska endured two decades of frustration following its trip to the Rose Bowl at the end of the 1940 season. Between then and Bob Devaney's arrival as head coach in 1962, the Cornhuskers enjoyed just three winning seasons, all of them under the direction of Bill Glassford, one of eight coaches during those twenty-one seasons. And even his seven-year tenure ended acrimoniously.

Nebraska's lack of success didn't indicate a lack of commitment or determination on the part of its players, however. Two, in particular, stood out, characterizing the spirit of a proud program for which losing, though never accepted, had become painfully commonplace.

The first was Tom Novak, a center and linebacker whose nickname captured the raw violence with which he played the game. He was known as "Trainwreck," and though his teams won only eleven of thirty-seven games in four seasons, he never made excuses, asking no quarter and giving none. And the second was Bobby Reynolds, a halfback who earned the nickname "Mr. Touchdown" in a remarkable sophomore season, but who was never able to duplicate that performance because of a series of injuries that ultimately prevented him from playing football or baseball professionally.

Both played for Glassford—Novak as a senior, Reynolds for three seasons. Both were homegrown—Novak from south Omaha, Reynolds from Grand Island. And both were links in an All-America chain that began with Vic Halligan, Guy Chamberlin, and Ed Weir in the early 1900s and continues today.

Tom Novak

The teams had returned to the field at Memorial Stadium on an unseasonably warm mid-November afternoon and the Cornhusker marching band was finishing its program at halftime of the final game of the 1949 season by forming the letters *T O M* and playing "Happy Birthday."

On the Nebraska sideline Tom Novak bent over to tighten a lace on his black, high-top, cleated shoes. He did so out of self-consciousness, *Lincoln Star* sports editor Norris Anderson later wrote. Novak was not given to public displays of sentiment. But he was touched by the band's tribute, which caused the crowd of 32,000 to stand and applaud the Cornhusker senior on the occasion of his twenty-fourth birthday. The applause came from both sides of the stadium, east and west; fans of Colorado—the afternoon's opponent—had joined in. Novak had a lump in his throat, wrote Anderson, who admitted that he, too, was overcome by the emotion of the moment. Had he swallowed twice, "the verdict might have been death by choking."

Had it only been a birthday tribute, there would have been no lumps. But Novak's career at Nebraska also was drawing to a close. Only thirty minutes, measured by the game clock on the face of Schulte Field House, remained.

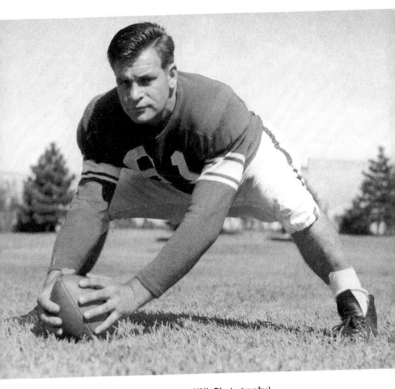

Trainwreck, Tom Novak. (Courtesy UNL Photography)

And then Novak would pull off his number 60 jersey for the final time.

For one player, on a team that would finish with a 4–5 record by defeating Colorado, to merit such a show of affection might seem out of the ordinary, particularly when his nickname was "Trainwreck." But there was nothing ordinary about Novak, anyway, as his evocative nickname suggested. A center and linebacker during his final three seasons, after trying fullback on offense as a freshman, he "was not just a great football player," Anderson wrote. "He was a beacon in

Twentieth Century's Best

Nearly 10,000 fans voted for players on Nebraska's team of the century, with Johnny Rodgers, the 1972 Heisman Trophy winner, receiving the most votes, 14,467. His votes included 7,358 as a wide receiver and 7,109 as a punt returner. Voting was conducted through April 2000.

Offense

WR Johnny Rodgers (1970–72)
WR Irving Fryar (1981–83)
TE Junior Miller (1977–79)
OT Bob Newton (1969–70)
OT Zach Wiegert (1991–94)
OG Will Shields (1989–92)
OG Dean Steinkuhler (1981–83)

OG/C Aaron Taylor (1994–97)
C Dave Rimington (1979–82)
QB Tommie Frazier (1992–95)
I-B Mike Rozier (1981–83)
I-B Roger Craig (1979–82)
FB Tom Rathman (1983–85)
FB Joel Makovicka (1995–98)

Defense

DE Grant Wistrom (1994–97)
DE/OLB Trev Alberts (1990–93)
DE/OLB Broderick Thomas (1985–88)
DT Jason Peter (1994–97)
DT Neil Smith (1985–87)
NT Rich Glover (1970–72)

LB Marc Munford (1984–86)
LB Ed Stewart (1991–94)
LB Tom Novak (1946–49)
CB Michael Booker (1994–96)
CB Ralph Brown (1996–99)
S Mike Brown (1996–99)
S Mike Minter (1993–96)

Special Teams

PK Kris Brown (1995–98)
P Jesse Kosch (1994–97)
KR Tyrone Hughes (1989–92)
PR Johnny Rodgers (1970–72)

the dark years, a promise for a brighter future and a symbol. His was the bridge on the Husker road back."

As it turned out, the bridge would span another decade. But Novak was a beacon and continues to be more than a half century later, shining brightly across the decades, defining the Nebraska spirit as few others before or since have. He was Cornhusker football distilled to its basic elements. "Victory or defeat, there was Novak, ever fierce, ever determined, savagely throwing that sturdy 205-pound body into play after play," wrote Anderson, who captured in words what now would be preserved on video. "No man ever gave more to Cornhusker football. Tom gave body, soul and unquenchable spirit. Novak's battering play sometimes took your breath away. . . . In the dressing room, you could see the toll. Face cut to ribbons, body a maze of bruises, there he would sit. Dejected, he'd be, but always with a 'there'll be a next year' if the cause was losing, a big grin if the day had been a winner."

There were few such days for Novak, whose teams lost far more often than not. He played for three coaches during his four years and the most successful was that last one, at 4–5. It might have been better, a winning season, Nebraska's first since 1940, if Glassford had made Novak the team's captain earlier. But Glassford, who was in his first season as the Cornhusker head coach, had followed his predecessors, naming captains on a game-by-game basis— until the sixth game against Missouri.

Nebraska went to Columbia with Novak as captain and nearly upset the Tigers, who were ranked number sixteen nationally in the Associated Press poll. The loss, by 21–20, was Nebraska's fourth in six games. The problem to that point in the season was that "the players didn't believe in themselves," Glassford said at a luncheon to honor the state's high school football champion in Omaha after the season. Then Novak served as the captain for the remaining three games, and through his leadership "the players suddenly found themselves," the AP quoted Glassford as saying. "They believed in themselves and felt they could win. And they did very well in those last four games [counting Missouri]."

Novak was accorded All-America recognition following his senior season, and he was a first-team all-conference selection in each of his four seasons, the only Cornhusker ever to be so honored. "I have seen lots of fine football players. But if I ever came to a life-or-death crossroads and had to name one player to carry the load for me, without hesitation I'd take Old Trainwreck," said Glassford.

Others shared Glassford's opinion of Novak. In the week following the Colorado game, Omaha businessman J. Gordon Roberts announced he was establishing an award in Novak's honor, to be presented annually to a senior football player at Nebraska who "best carried on the high type of play and leadership exhibited by Tom Novak." The award has been presented every year, beginning in 1951.

In addition, the Cornhusker lettermen's club retired the number 60 jersey Novak wore as a senior—he wore a number 68 jersey as a freshman and sophomore and a number 61 jersey as a junior. Nebraska would retire other jersey numbers in later years, based on players winning major national awards, beginning with Heisman Trophy winner Johnny Rodgers's number 20 and Outland Trophy and Lombardi Award winner Rich Glover's number 79 following the 1972 season. But with duplicate numbers now a problem because of the size of the squad, only the players' jerseys are retired, except for Novak's number 60. "I didn't think much about it at the time," Novak once said of his number being retired by the N Club. As the years went by, however, it made him feel "pretty darn good."

Novak also played baseball, earning three letters as a catcher and contributing to Big Seven Conference championships in 1948 and 1950. But football was his sport. And he was determined to succeed from the time he played football for Coach Cornie Collin at South High School in Omaha. After seeing a newspaper photograph of himself pursuing a ball carrier from Benson High, Novak decided that would be the first of many times his picture or at least his name was going to be in the newspaper. "I drove myself into the scrapbook," he would say many years later.

He was a World War II veteran when he enrolled at Nebraska, after visiting Notre Dame, where he might have gone if Fighting Irish coach Frank Leahy, a native of O'Neill, Nebraska, had allowed him to scrimmage with the players during his visit. But Leahy insisted that he commit to Notre Dame first, so he returned to Omaha and discussed the matter with Collin. His high school coach, who had given him his colorful nickname, told him that South Bend, Indiana, was too far away, that he should stay close to home so his parents could watch him play. Collin gave him some additional advice, as well. He should stay out of pool halls and movie theaters, Collin said, and he shouldn't buy a car. So Novak hitchhiked home while he was at Nebraska— finding rides was never difficult when he was wearing his Cornhusker letter sweater—and if he had a speaking engagement, for which he could earn as much as $50, he would check out a vehicle from the university motor pool.

In 1947, when Novak was a sophomore, Nebraska traveled to South Bend to play a Notre Dame team that would finish the season 9–0 and earn the AP national championship. Though Leahy's heavily favored Fighting Irish won 31–0, Novak earned the respect of those who watched him that afternoon. According to one newspaper account, he made seventeen tackles during a twenty-one-play span. "From a Nebraska standpoint, the game is a story about one player," the account said. Novak was that player.

He had been the game captain and on the team's return to Lincoln, he addressed the crowd estimated at 1,000 that had come to the Burlington train station on a Monday morning to welcome him and his teammates. Despite the outcome his spirit hadn't been broken. "They weren't as tough as I thought they would be," he said, speaking into a bullhorn, hands in his pockets, above the cheering. That was "Trainwreck" Novak. Lyell Bremser, the longtime radio voice of Cornhusker football and a legendary figure himself, once said: "My eyes have never seen Tom Novak's equal at any position. As football players go, the Good Lord made Tom Novak then threw away the mold."

Bobby Reynolds

Nebraska earned the respect of those who watched in the Orange Bowl stadium that warm night in early December 1951, despite the score. The Cornhuskers "fought as though defeat were a stranger to them, instead of a companion," a *Miami Herald* reporter would write after the 19–7 loss against a heavily favored Miami team that had recently accepted a bid to play in the Gator Bowl.

Nebraska, in contrast, had endured a "dismal" season, the reporter noted. And he was being kind. The loss was the Cornhuskers' eighth in a season that had begun with such

Mr. Touchdown, Bobby Reynolds. (Courtesy UNL Photography)

promise. They had been number twelve in the Associated Press national rankings when they opened at home against TCU, coming off a 1950 season in which they had finished with their first winning record since 1940, 6–2–1.

The optimism had quickly faded, however, leaving them to play for nothing more than pride in the first night game in school history, before a partisan Miami crowd of 32,283, which had come expecting the Hurricanes to cover the four-touchdown betting line—for entertainment purposes only. Instead, what the fans saw was a courageous Cornhusker effort that might have produced an upset if not for a six-minute stretch at the beginning of the second half, during which Miami scored thirteen points. And they came away as impressed with Bobby Reynolds as the *Miami Herald* reporter had been. "The Hurricanes beat Nebraska as a unit but they didn't beat Reynolds as a man," he wrote. Even taking into consideration the tendency toward hyperbole of sports writers at that time, the Reynolds performance was noteworthy. He rushed for 174 yards. He passed for 57 yards. He returned kicks. He punted. And he scored the only Cornhusker touchdown, on a 10-yard pass reception.

When he was on the sideline, he held ice on his left eye because of a recently burned cornea. The cornea had been burned by lime used to mark the lines on a football field. The injury, which threatened the sight in the eye, wasn't his only one that season. He missed the first three games because of a shoulder separation, suffered during Coach Bill Glassford's rugged preseason training camp, conducted far away from Lincoln at the university's agricultural college in Curtis, Nebraska. During two-a-day practices in the late-summer heat, three tacklers had piled on the 5'11", 175-pound Reynolds.

Reynolds's Run

Bobby Reynolds had an uncanny knack of setting up blocks as evidenced on the most famous touchdown run of his career against Missouri at Memorial Stadium in 1950. The Cornhuskers faced fourth down and short yardage at the Missouri 33 yard line with six minutes remaining. Bob Broeg of the *St. Louis Post-Dispatch* wrote: "He hand-faked one guy, swivel-hipped another and set out for the goal now 60 crow-flight yards away. He picked up three nice blocks, stepped away from another tackler and took advantage of two more blocks. It was an astounding run. The kid stands out like a neon light."

One of Reynolds's blockers, 6', 220-pound tackle Charles Toogood, knocked down a Tiger defender and wouldn't allow him to get up. "The play's over," the Missouri player pleaded. "Not necessarily," Toogood replied. "He might come back this way again."

Afterward, the modest Reynolds said the play was "dumb" and he should have passed.

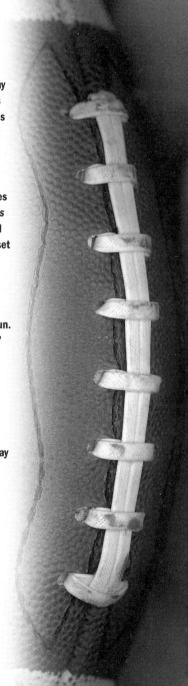

The shoulder separation, one of two during his career, set the tone for a junior season in which great expectations for him, as well as for his team, would turn to talk of what might have been. And the performance against Miami provided tangible evidence of such coffee shop speculation.

Even with victory out of reach, Reynolds and his teammates refused to fold. As time ran out, the Cornhuskers moved deep into Miami territory, on a 40-yard Reynolds pass and an 18-yard Reynolds run, both out of Glassford's spread offense. The game ended at the Hurricanes' 2 yard line. Afterward, Reynolds credited his blockers for his rushing success, asking writers to be sure to mention them, and attributed the touchdown reception of a deflected pass to his being "awful lucky," in the right place at the right time. He wore such modesty like his number 12 jersey.

Nebraska's collapse in 1951 was a result of several factors, many of them involving backfield players. Nick Adduci, a starting fullback in 1949 and 1950, was inducted into the Army prior to the season. Don Vogt quit the team, and Tom Carrodine was dismissed from it. In addition quarterback Johnny Bordogna was slowed by an ankle injury. But the health of Reynolds was the key.

He burst on the scene as a sophomore, earning All-America recognition and the nickname "Mr. Touchdown" — a profile published in *Collier's* magazine in late September 1951 made the nickname national — after leading the nation in scoring with 22 touchdowns and 157 points. He was chosen to the Grantland Rice *Look* magazine All-America team, the first to be presented on television. Someone quipped, however, there were so few television sets in Nebraska that not many were able to watch.

Reynolds also set a Cornhusker single-season record by rushing for 1,342 yards. Mike Rozier wouldn't break the record until the ninth game of the 1982 season, gaining 251 yards against Oklahoma State. The record had lasted for so long, thirty-two years, that Rozier didn't know who had held it. After the Oklahoma State game, with Reynolds in the locker room for a photo opportunity, Rozier told reporters he figured a more recent Nebraska I-back, Isaiah Hipp or Jarvis Redwine, had held the record.

Reynolds's ability as a running back depended on more than speed, although he had that. As a baseball player, he led the Big Seven Conference in stolen bases his sophomore year. But he also had an uncanny knack of utilizing his blockers, setting them up, and then reacting to what they did. And he was always quick to acknowledge their efforts. Scoring a touchdown was a result of "a chain of circumstances" involving everyone on the field, he was once quoted as saying. "Very often, the fellow who carries the ball across the goal line is the least important link in the whole chain."

He was as humble as he was athletically talented, and his talents were evident not only in football but also in baseball, the sport in which he most likely would have had a professional future if not for the football injuries and a broken leg suffered sliding into home plate during his senior baseball season. His success in baseball was such that the *Collier's* profile reported that not only did he keep a Ted Williams model bat in his room at the university and handle it while he studied, but also that he had turned down a sizeable bonus offer from the Chicago White Sox out of high school. He was able to turn down the offer, the story said, because his grandfather had left him a good deal of money.

He had attended a New York Yankees tryout in Branson, Missouri, in 1949, prior to his freshman year at Nebraska. Among those at the tryout, he would recall years later, was a young, would-be shortstop from Commerce, Oklahoma, named Mickey Mantle. But it wasn't true that he kept a bat in his room, he said. His fraternity brothers would have made fun of him. And his grandfather didn't leave him a fortune.

His maternal grandfather, Charles Olson, did have an impact on the university, however. His construction company built the student union, the library, and the engineering hall. And his parents had been involved in athletics at Nebraska. His mom, Blenda, was the captain of the senior girls basketball team in 1925, and his dad, Gil, was a third-string halfback on Coach Fred Dawson's 1923 Cornhusker football team.

Reynolds was born in Omaha but grew up in Grand Island, where his family moved when he was two years old. By his senior year in high school, his name was familiar statewide because of his athletic accomplishments. He excelled as an infielder in American Legion baseball. He first qualified for the state high school track and field meet as a sophomore. And he played for basketball teams that were a combined 44–1 and won consecutive state championships in his sophomore and junior years.

Again, the *Collier's* profile was off the mark, describing him as a high school basketball player who had gone to Nebraska as an "unheralded football player." Unheralded? Hardly. When he was a junior in 1947, Grand Island High's football game against Lincoln High in Lincoln was moved to Nebraska's Memorial Stadium, where an estimated 15,000 to 20,000 watched his Islanders win 25–14. His

Old-Time All-Time Team

Acknowledging college football's one-hundredth anniversary in 1969, fans voted on an all-time Nebraska team, using ballots in game programs. Only one player made this team and the Cornhuskers all-century team selected in 2000, center-linebacker Tom Novak.

Ends
Guy Chamberlin (1914–15)
Clarence Swanson (1918–21)
Freeman White (1963–65)
Tony Jeter (1963–65)

Tackles
Roy "Link" Lyman (1918–21)
Ed Weir (1923–25)
Charles Toogood (1947–50)
Walt Barnes (1963–65)

Guards
Warren Alfson (1938–40)
Ed Husmann (1950–52)
Bob Brown (1961–63)
Wayne Meylan (1965–67)

Centers
Charles Brock (1936–38)
Tom Novak (1946–49)

Quarterbacks
Bernie Masterson (1931–33)
Dennis Claridge (1961–63)

Halfbacks
Lloyd Cardwell (1934–36)
Bobby Reynolds (1950–52)
Kent McCloughan (1962–64)
Larry Wachholtz (1964–66)

Fullbacks
George Sauer (1931–33)
Sam Francis (1934–36)

exploits on the football field were such that Phog Allen, the legendary basketball coach at Kansas, created a controversy in the spring of 1951 by announcing at a banquet in New York City that an unidentified school had offered Reynolds $10,000 and a Cadillac as recruiting inducements, raising the question of what Nebraska had offered. Cornhusker Athletic Director George "Potsy" Clark, who had coached at Kansas, told the *Lincoln Journal* that the comments were "Phog's annual speech to get himself quoted in the papers." Allen claimed that "the whole thing was a mistake," the *Journal* reported. Mistake or not, cynics could believe Reynolds had such value, given his performance in 1950.

That one season effectively defined his career. Because of the injuries, he played in only thirteen games during his final two seasons, rushing for 854 yards and scoring 54 points. But when Nebraska picked an all-time team, in conjunction with college football's one-hundredth anniversary in 1969, he was on it.

When he died in August 1985, the *Lincoln Journal* compared him with Notre Dame's George Gipp and Iowa's Nile Kinnick in filling a "mythological spot" in Cornhusker football. He would always be Nebraska's "transcendent football hero." The headline read: "So Long, Mr. Touchdown."

Double Hundred

All 3,200 tickets were sold, and comedian Bob Hope was the featured speaker. The audience on the floor of the Bob Devaney Sports Center arena included Nebraska governor Bob Kerrey and United States senators J. J. Exon and Ed Zorinsky, as well as numerous Cornhusker football All-Americans. The occasion, held in early December of 1983, was the Double Hundred Celebration, honoring former Nebraska head coach Bob Devaney, the athletic director at the time, and the then-current Cornhusker coach Tom Osborne. The two were the first major college football coaches to reach one hundred victories in consecutive careers at the same school, an achievement that would "stand tall in the folklore of a sport that cherishes its magicians and traditions," wrote the *Omaha World-Herald's* Wally Provost.

Devaney coached victory number one hundred in the last of his eleven seasons at Nebraska. A 52-yard punt return for a touchdown by Johnny Rodgers opened the scoring in a thirty-eight-point first half as the Cornhuskers rolled over Kansas State 59–7, in the next-to-last game of the 1972 regular season.

Devaney had intended to step aside as head coach following the 1971 season but was persuaded to remain in an attempt to win an unprecedented third consecutive national championship. A 23–23 tie with Iowa State the week before the Kansas State game, however, ended that quest. A loss to Oklahoma and a decisive victory over Notre

The 1995 national championship defense included Grant Wistrom (left) and brothers Christian Peter (55) and Jason Peter (95). (Courtesy Huskers Illustrated)

Dame in the Orange Bowl game would give him a 101–20–2 record at Nebraska, to go with the national titles in 1970 and 1971, and establish a standard by which Osborne, his handpicked successor, would be measured.

Osborne proved up to the task. The fourth game of his eleventh season as head coach in 1983 was victory number one hundred, 48–14 over UCLA. There was symmetry to it given that his first victory, in his first game as head coach in 1973, also came at the Bruins' expense. During twenty-five seasons as coach, Osborne's teams would go 255–49–3 and win three national titles in his final four seasons—the last 1997.

The Cornhuskers appeared to be headed for a national championship in 1983, when the Double Hundred Celebration was held. They had swept through the regular season with an offense that had been nicknamed "The Scoring Explosion," ranked number one in the polls from beginning to end. Some considered them the best college football team ever assembled. On the night of January 2, 1984, however, Miami upset them 31–30 in the Orange Bowl game, when Osborne elected to go for a two-point conversion at the game's end rather than settle for a kick for an almost-certain extra point and tie, which probably would have meant the title.

The decision to go for two points and the victory defined Osborne's coaching career from a national point of view. George Vecsey of the *New York Times* wrote afterward, "Osborne showed that he and his team and his college and his state loved winning so much that they would take the chance of losing." Milton Richman of United Press International echoed Vecsey: "The Nebraska Cornhuskers lost the game, but not their dignity," he wrote. "For that, they can thank their coach, Tom Osborne. No other coach embodied good coaching principles more or served as a better model of correctitude to his players."

In the days following the game, Osborne received more than 1,000 letters, most of them commending him on his courage in playing to win. "I don't think I could have gone in the locker room and looked at those players with the idea we didn't try to win," he said. "It may have been a foolhardy thing to do. I guess hindsight is always 20–20, but I think it was the right thing to do. There's no question in my mind that if we had to do it over again, we would do the same thing."

His first national championship wouldn't happen until victory number 219, against Miami in the 1995 Orange Bowl game (24–17). His attitude hadn't changed. "I've never won a game," he told reporters following victory number one hundred. "I say that very seriously. The players win games."

Bob Devaney

Nebraska football was "mired in a dismal swamp of frustration and despair," the *Omaha World-Herald*'s Wally Provost would write years later, characterizing the 1940s and 1950s. The Cornhuskers managed only three winning seasons from 1941 through 1961, and when Bill Jennings was fired as coach following a 3–6–1 record in 1961, Nebraska fans had endured six successive losing seasons. Five of those seasons had been under Jennings, the sixth under Pete Elliott, the youngest head coach in Cornhusker history at age twenty-nine. Elliott came from Oklahoma, where he was an assistant to the legendary Bud Wilkinson, and spent only one season at Nebraska before leaving to coach at California. Jennings, also a former Wilkinson assistant, joined Elliott's staff, leaving a job in the oil business.

Jennings was popular among fans and players alike when he replaced Elliott. But he didn't have sufficient on-field talent for immediate success. The "cupboard was bare," Clete Fischer would recall. A Cornhusker letterman in the late 1940s under George "Potsy" Clark, Bernie Masterson, and then Clark again, Fischer joined the Jennings staff in 1959 and remained an assistant at Nebraska until retiring in 1985. As the losses mounted, Jennings's popularity diminished, and he began to drive his

No Refund

Bob Devaney's coaching tenure might have been brief if Miami could have been more persuasive. In December of 1963, as Devaney began preparing his team for an Orange Bowl battle with Auburn, the Hurricanes tried to entice him to become head coach, replacing Andy Gustafson, who was stepping aside to become athletic director. Reportedly, Miami was ready to offer the forty-eight-year-old Devaney an annual salary of $25,000 to relocate to southern Florida. Devaney earned $19,000 a year at Nebraska.

Despite rumors that some Cornhusker assistants had put their homes up for sale and that his son Mike had requested a transfer from the Nebraska chapter of his fraternity to the one at Miami, Devaney stayed. In explaining the decision he joked that wife Phyllis had just bought snow tires and couldn't get her money back.

players harder and harder, taking the approach that more is better. The team would be on the practice field at 3:30 in the afternoon and not leave it until 7:30 or 8:00, often scrimmaging much of the time.

The Cornhuskers managed some upsets under his direction, 14–6 over fourteenth-ranked Pittsburgh in the final home game in 1958, 14–13 over number four Texas at Austin in the 1960 season opener, and 25–21 over Oklahoma at Memorial Stadium on Halloween in 1959, a victory among the most memorable in school history. Even though Wilkinson's Sooners had lost twice and were only ranked number nineteen, they previously had gone seventy-four consecutive conference games without defeat, dating to the 1946 season.

Nebraska defeated Oklahoma again the next season, at Norman, but Jennings angered fans by comments he made in speaking to boosters in Omaha. Among other things, he criticized fans for their lack of support and questioned the talent the state's high schools produced, or at least, that's how what he said was taken. An editorial in the university student newspaper said that he had "bought a one-way ticket back to private business, unless some other school wants him," and there were calls for his resignation.

Jennings, who claimed his remarks had been misinterpreted, didn't resign. But he couldn't survive another losing season, which a Lincoln newspaper summed up as "bad weather, bad team, bad schedule." Five days after a 21–14 loss against Oklahoma in the final game of 1961 before the second-smallest home crowd of the season, a disappointing 26,139, Chancellor Clifford Hardin fired him. Hardin handled the firing because Nebraska had been without an athletic director for a year, following the departure of Bill Orwig. Joseph Soshnik and Charles Miller had shared duties during the interim. The day after Jennings was fired, Hardin hired William "Tippy" Dye as the Cornhuskers' new athletic director, at an annual salary of $18,500. Frank Morrison, the state's governor, had a salary of $14,000.

A little over a month later, forty-five-year-old Bob Devaney arrived from Wyoming to lead Nebraska football to national prominence, achieving immediate success with players Jennings had recruited. Nebraska's facilities didn't even match Wyoming's, but Devaney and his assistants were impressed by the size and speed of the players. When he and Jennings met, in a cramped office on the second floor of the Coliseum, Devaney told his predecessor that if he, Jennings, were to stay another season, he would win.

"We were far from starting from scratch. There were good players here," Devaney said later. Professional teams would draft twelve of the forty-nine Cornhuskers who suited up for the opening game against South Dakota in 1962. And there also was a commitment to win. Clarence Swanson, the head of the Board of Regents, convinced him of that. On the trip back to Wyoming after visiting with Hardin and Swanson, Devaney told Jim Ross, a Wyoming assistant and longtime friend, that they could win at Nebraska.

Michigan State's coach, Duffy Daugherty, for whom Devaney had been an assistant, also encouraged him to take the job. He could win a national championship at Nebraska, Daugherty said, something he couldn't do at Wyoming. Daugherty had recommended Devaney to Hardin, a former agriculture professor at Michigan State, after Hardin contacted Daugherty on the outside chance he might be interested in the job.

The new AD, "Tippy" Dye, came from what is now Wichita State, however, and his first choice as Jennings' replacement was Hank Foldberg, who had been the Wheat-shockers' football coach. Foldberg played collegiately at both Texas A&M and Army, where he was a teammate of Doc Blanchard and Glenn Davis. He turned down Dye's offer, taking the job as athletic director and football coach at A&M instead, opening the opportunity for Devaney, one of three finalists after Foldberg, all from the Skyline Conference.

Included in initial speculation about the coaching choice were NFL great Otto Graham; former Los Angeles Rams head coach Bob Snyder; Boys Town, Nebraska, High School coach Maurice "Skip" Palrang; and Fischer, who was endorsed by ten high school coaches in Omaha. There were others from the college ranks, among them Iowa

After 6–4 records in 1967 and 1968, boosters in Omaha circulated a petition to get rid of Bob Devaney. In 1970 and 1971, his teams won national championships, the first in school history. (Courtesy UNL Photography)

State's Clay Stapleton, Ohio's Bill Hess, Arizona's Jim LaRue, Detroit's Jim Miller, and Virginia's Bill Elias. But Utah's Ray Nagel, Utah State's John Ralston, and Devaney would emerge as leading contenders.

Although Ralston was considered the front-runner in media speculation, Devaney, who registered at a Lincoln hotel under an assumed name during a visit to meet with Dye, was the choice. By late December newspapers in Laramie and Cheyenne were reporting that Wyoming's fifth-year coach would be heading for Nebraska. That was easier said than done, however, because Devaney would have to break what was loosely described as a "lifetime" contract with Wyoming in order to take the job. He was busy laying the groundwork at Nebraska nearly a month before Wyoming reluctantly released him.

Being a temporary stop for successful coaches frustrated Wyoming. But it also knew what it had in Devaney, whose teams were a combined 35–10–5 in five seasons. His ability to recruit served him well in Laramie, as it would at Nebraska. Like Daugherty, his mentor, Devaney's Irish wit and charm appealed not only to the athletes he recruited but also to their parents. "He recruited my mom," recalled Dave Morock, a starting defensive back on Nebraska's first national championship team in 1970. Devaney joked that recruiting the mom was critical, but that one time, a coach did such a good job the mom enrolled and the son went elsewhere. After Morock got to Nebraska, Devaney would "go out of his way to ask, 'How's Rose?'" Morock said. "Not just, 'How's your mom?' but, 'How's Rose?'"

Players related to Devaney because of his blue-collar background. He grew up in Saginaw, Michigan, the son of a sailor on Great Lakes iron ore boats, and worked in a

First Bowl Victory

The Gotham Bowl is barely a footnote in college football history. The game was played only twice. What would have been the first, in 1960, was canceled because of an inability to get two teams willing to go to New York City in December to play. Baylor defeated Utah State 24-9 at the Polo Grounds on a bitterly cold afternoon a year later, before a disappointing crowd estimated at 15,000. Officials were optimistic the 1962 game, a benefit for the March of Dimes, would attract a larger crowd, perhaps 30,000.

The optimism was based on several factors, including a switch in venue to Yankee Stadium, which was more accessible than the Polo Grounds—though the facilities were just across the Harlem River from each other—and the intersectional matchup between Nebraska and Miami.

Nebraska's acceptance was something of a surprise. A Lincoln newspaper reported that "minor bowls," specifically the Gotham and Liberty Bowls, had been "ruled out" by the Cornhuskers, who had seen hopes of representing the Big Eight Conference in the Orange Bowl vanish in a 34-6 loss at Oklahoma in the final game of the regular season. But Nebraska had made only two bowl appearances in its history and both had resulted in losses. So when the Gotham Bowl extended an invitation, the players voted unanimously to accept, despite the reservations of first-year Coach Bob Devaney and his staff. Because the bowl was plagued by financial difficulties, Nebraska didn't head east until the day before the game, waiting at the Lincoln airport with bags packed until Gotham Bowl officials placed a certified check in escrow to cover the team's travel expenses.

The turf was frozen, with most players wearing tennis shoes for better footing. The Cornhuskers won 36-34, before a crowd generously estimated at 11,000, with only 6,166 paid. If 11,000 had showed up, then 10,000 must have gone home before the game began, Devaney would recall years later. So few attended that copies of the Gotham Bowl program fetch top dollar on the memorabilia market today.

Chevrolet foundry for three years following high school before enrolling at Alma College. He summarized that background in a locker room speech to his team prior to the 1962 Gotham Bowl game in New York City. Yankee Stadium was nearly empty and the temperature was around twenty degrees. "I told the players that the weather was terrible and the game didn't seem like a very big deal because nobody was out there," he wrote in his 1981 autobiography. "Then I said it reminded me of the days when I was a kid and we used to have fights in the back alley. There wouldn't be anyone watching there either, but pride was still the most important thing in the world."

Sports Illustrated's John Underwood described Devaney—who said his name rhymed with "fanny"—as "unpretentious" and "unassuming," with a "broad, pleasant potato face" and a "dumpy baker's build." *Newsweek* magazine said he resembled "Wallace Beery rather than Kirk Douglas." However he might have looked to those who didn't know him, he was a tough competitor; he had been an amateur boxer as well as a football player. He was organized. He delegated responsibility to well-chosen assistants. And he could motivate and relate to "tough guys from the steel mills, guys [that] had to fight to survive," said Larry Kramer, an All-American at tackle in 1964, who had been recruited by Jennings.

After the lengthy and physically debilitating practices run by Jennings, Devaney's were a breath of fresh air. "You learned through repetition," Kramer said. "He was not a guy who would scrimmage every day, just a lot of repetition. He had a subtle way to do it. He was not a guy who was a screamer or a hollerer."

Devaney had a temper, however, and left no doubt when he was unhappy. Joe Blahak, a starter in the secondary on the back-to-back national championship teams, learned that as a sophomore. On a third-and-long situation, he broke on a receiver running a curl route, thinking interception. His aggressiveness left another receiver open, however, and if not for a tackle by safety Bill Kosch, the play would have produced a touchdown instead of a first down. Rather than coming off the field by the most direct route, Blahak angled as far away from Devaney as he could, seeking solace among some linemen. Suddenly the linemen parted and there was Devaney, his face as red as his cap and jacket. "You couldn't tell where either of them ended and his face began," Blahak said years later. "He grabbed my face mask and told me in words only he could put together if I ever did that again, I'd never play another down at Nebraska."

Nebraska had enjoyed success before Devaney, going back to the early 1900s. During D. X. Bible's tenure as coach, from 1929 through 1936, the Cornhuskers were a combined 50–15–7 and won six conference titles. And in the four seasons before that, under Fred Dawson, they won three. Devaney, who never coached a team with a losing record at any level, resurrected Nebraska's tradition, lifting the program from the "dismal swamp of frustration and despair" and taking it to another level.

After completing his eligibility, Morock was playing in a charity basketball game with other former Cornhuskers when a spectator said, "You guys created a monster." The monster was the first national title, which was followed by another the next season. They became the standard for Devaney's successor.

Tom Osborne

In early December of 1978, Tom Osborne made one of the most significant decisions in Cornhusker football history. He decided to remain at Nebraska, turning down a reported $100,000 annual salary to replace a fired Bill Mallory as the head coach at Colorado. On a conference call from Kansas City International Airport, where he had flown from Denver after visiting the Colorado campus and meeting with players he would have coached, Osborne told reporters in Nebraska that he was staying.

Had the decision been a "plain business proposition, I'd have gone to Colorado," he said. His salary in his sixth year as Nebraska's head coach was $36,040. Plus, the pressure to win wouldn't have been as great at Colorado, not immediately anyway. But "when I thought of the players we had recruited at Nebraska, it would be very difficult to tell them that I was going to go and coach against them." So he turned down the offer and immediately left to go recruiting. Hence, the conference call. "I wasn't bluffing," Osborne would say of the visit to Boulder years later. "I really thought I would take the job when I went out there." Wife Nancy even made the trip with him.

Osborne didn't seek the job. The initial contact came from Colorado track and field coach Dean Brittenham, a former assistant at Nebraska. Brittenham, a friend, asked if Osborne had any interest in talking to Athletic Director Eddie Crowder, whose first choice to replace Mallory reportedly was former Oklahoma coach Bud Wilkinson, the head coach of the NFL's St. Louis Cardinals at the time. Crowder had played quarterback and safety for Wilkinson at Oklahoma in the early 1950s.

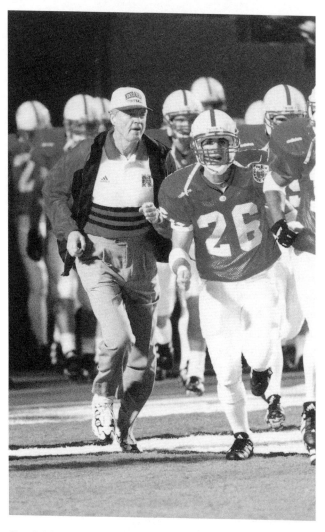

Tom Osborne's final five teams had a combined record of 60–3, with three national championships. (*Courtesy* Huskers Illustrated)

Failing to coax Wilkinson to Boulder, Crowder turned his attention to other candidates. Even though the forty-year-old Osborne had compiled a 55–15–2 record as Bob Devaney's handpicked successor, five of the losses had been against Oklahoma, by a combined score of 148–48. Less than a month before his visit to Boulder, Osborne's Cornhuskers had defeated Oklahoma for the first time since 1971. The losses to Oklahoma "got to be kind of an obsession with our fans," he would say later.

Oklahoma wasn't the only reason he considered leaving, however. An Omaha television station had dropped his weekly coach's show. Though the cancellation wouldn't affect his income from the syndicated show—his decisions weren't based on financial considerations—it could affect recruiting. And that was a concern, as well as an indication that he might have been underappreciated.

The Colorado job was also appealing because Osborne was an avid fisherman, dating to his childhood in Hastings, Nebraska, and evidenced by the 38-inch, 31-pound king salmon mounted on the wall of his office. He had pulled the fish from Lake Michigan in 1978. Fishing "always kind of relaxed me," he said. And Colorado offered good fishing.

Replacing Devaney had been no small task. In addition to his .829 winning percentage, Devaney's final three teams were a combined 33–2–2, with back-to-back national championships. And during his eleven seasons, Nebraska had won eight conference championships, seven outright. Given that remarkable success, to which Osborne contributed as an assistant, "I felt when I took over for Bob it would be uphill," Osborne said. "I thought it would be difficult to last more than five years. Bob always had a built-in grace factor because he turned the program around. I wasn't going to have that opportunity because I was more of a caretaker."

Osborne never intended to be the head coach at Nebraska. He never intended to be a head coach anywhere when he contacted Devaney about becoming a graduate assistant following his retirement from a brief career in the National Football League. He had been an eighteenth-round draft pick of the San Francisco 49ers out of Hastings College, where he was a two-time state college athlete of the year, and played two seasons as a wide receiver for the Washington Redskins after a season on the 49ers' taxi squad.

He played quarterback in college, but San Francisco's Coach Red Hickey moved him to receiver. He was second on the Redskins in receptions in 1961, with 22 for 297 yards and 2 touchdowns. But he had pulled a hamstring running the 40-yard dash during training camp and continued to play with the injury, which worsened to the point that he decided to end his career and return to school to continue graduate studies.

Osborne had begun graduate work at Southern California during the off-season and supervised the dorm that housed Coach John McKay's freshman football players. Instead of continuing at USC, however, he went home to Nebraska. Devaney had been hired but hadn't relocated to Lincoln yet, so Osborne sent a letter to the new Cornhusker head coach in care of the Wyoming athletic department.

Devaney offered Osborne meals at the training table and a room at Selleck Quadrangle, where he would monitor athletes who lived there, specifically the "rowdies," recalled Larry Kramer, who was among them. "We were the 'uglies.'" Osborne's job was to keep them in line, break up fights, and in one case intercede on the behalf of a player who was

And You Are?

Tom Osborne's relationship with his players was a key to his success. He earned their respect, according to Jon Hesse, who lettered at linebacker from 1994 to 1996. One day, Hesse and some other veteran players were on the South Stadium elevator with Osborne and a freshman walk-on, whose name Hesse didn't know. After joking with the veterans, Osborne turned to the small-town walk-on, acknowledged him by name, and congratulated him on the fact that his high school team had defeated its rival the previous weekend. "I thought then, 'That's why he's the man,' " Hesse said, recalling the encounter. "I had no idea who he was. But Coach Osborne did. Those things happened quite often."

about to be expelled for throwing snowballs at passing motorists and lifting newspapers from outside the doors of other dorm rooms. Osborne also coached the freshman receivers for two seasons, before moving up to the varsity receivers in 1964.

When he took the graduate assistant's position he had considered it as a way of easing out of football. He hadn't intended for it to lead to a career in coaching. But after dividing his time for two years between coaching and teaching in the Department of Educational Psychology and Measurements—in which he earned a Ph.D.—he settled on coaching. During that time he looked into a coaching and teaching position at Augustana College and a head coaching position at South Dakota.

After the 1969 season, he was a candidate for the head coaching position at Texas Tech, again finishing second, this time to Jim Carlen, who had head coaching experience at West Virginia. By then Devaney had discussed the possibility of Osborne's stepping in at Nebraska when he, Devaney, retired. After the fan unrest that followed 6–4 records in 1967 and 1968, Devaney gave Osborne the responsibility of restructuring the offense, which had been based on the T formation, with an unbalanced line. Osborne installed an I-formation offense, with slotback and spread alignments.

Though he continued to work with the receivers, Osborne also began meeting with the quarterbacks every day at the training table. He "covered everything in those meetings," said Jerry Tagge, a quarterback on the 1970 and 1971 national championship teams. "He was thorough. He just didn't leave anything uncovered. 'Here's how we're going to attack them.' It was really educational. He didn't waste your time. He came prepared. He didn't just show up and start drawing on the chalkboard."

Osborne was the offensive mastermind behind the back-to-back national championship teams, calling the plays from the press box. And even though he didn't have the same perspective at field level, he continued to coordinate the offense throughout his twenty-five seasons as head coach. "I'd say from 1969 on, he called every offensive snap," said Guy Ingles, who lettered at wide receiver from 1968 through 1970.

Devaney decided he would retire and turn over the program to Osborne following the 1971 season. He could do that because he was the athletic director; he had been since 1967. But he was persuaded to remain in 1972 to pursue a third consecutive national championship, delaying Osborne's promotion one year. During that season Osborne carried the title assistant head coach.

Osborne had other opportunities during his twenty-five seasons as head coach, including a couple of jobs in the NFL, with the Houston Oilers and the Seattle Seahawks, the second being the more attractive of the two. But the Colorado job was the one he came closest to taking. He discussed the possibility with his assistants because he would have taken them with him. And they encouraged him to investigate it. "I would not have even taken a visit if I wasn't serious," Osborne said, looking back after he had retired.

His going to Boulder would have changed Cornhusker history dramatically, not only because he wouldn't have been directing Nebraska but also because his replacement would have had to coach against him each season in conference play. All of his teams won at least nine games and went to bowls. They won thirteen conference titles, including nine outright, and three national championships. And in 1998, with the waiting period waived, he was inducted into the College Football Hall of Fame, joining Devaney.

Throughout his coaching career, all thirty-six years at Nebraska, Osborne focused on the journey rather than the destination. "Trophies and whistles and bells and rings don't excite me that much," he said.

Game of the Century

Opposition to the Vietnam War and social injustice continued to cause unrest on the nation's college campuses, though the involvement of the United States in the war was winding down. The U.S. command had announced its lowest weekly casualty toll since combat troops arrived in Vietnam six years earlier. The most recent issue of Life magazine included a story about the ongoing pullout of troops.

In addition to the war, national headlines told of inmates at the state prison in Rahway, New Jersey, taking the warden and four guards hostage. Two months earlier, state troopers had been called in to quell a riot at a prison in Attica, New York. The People's Republic of China had just been seated at the United Nations for the first time. *Marcus Welby, M.D.* and *Gunsmoke* were among the most popular shows on television. And *Billboard*'s number one single that week was the "Theme from Shaft."

That morning in New York City, the annual Macy's Thanksgiving Day parade had been without its giant balloon figures, which were to include the unveiling of a new Mickey Mouse. But Mickey and his helium-filled friends might have sailed away in a twenty-mile-per-hour wind, gusting to forty. Even though rain fell on the parade, held in near-freezing temperatures, it could have been worse. Heavy rains in Philadelphia caused the cancellation of the Gimbel's parade.

The date was November 25, 1971, and for the better part of the afternoon, at least, the attention of college football fans, in particular those of Nebraska and Oklahoma, was on Owen Field in Norman, Oklahoma, where a sellout crowd of more than 61,000 watched the number one Cornhuskers drive 74 yards to a touchdown in the closing minutes to defeat the second-ranked Sooners, 35–31.

Interest in the game had begun to build early in the season when it became apparent that neither team ran even a remote risk of losing until the day Nebraska's Blackshirt defense would finally face Oklahoma's Wishbone T offense. The *Sports Illustrated* issue the week of the game featured a cover on which Sooner halfback Greg Pruitt and Cornhusker linebacker Bob Terrio were positioned face mask to face mask, beneath the headline: "Irresistible Oklahoma Meets Immovable Nebraska." Nebraska led the nation in total defense and scoring defense, while Oklahoma led the nation in total offense, rushing offense, and scoring offense. Through nine games, the Sooners had averaged 563 total yards, including 481 on the ground, and 45 points. In 10 games Nebraska had allowed, on average, only 172 total yards and 6.4 points—while gaining 441 yards and scoring 38.9 points.

It would be the "Game of the Century," an appellation most recently applied to the Texas–Arkansas game on December 6, 1969, according to *Sports Illustrated*. Texas and Arkansas both had taken 9–0 records into the game. The Longhorns won 15–14 and went on to be named national champions in the major polls, with Arkansas finishing third in one and seventh in the other. *Sports Illustrated*'s list of twenty-five games of the century candidates included two ties, Michigan State–Notre Dame (10–10) in 1966 and Notre Dame–Army (0–0) in 1946.

Although the Cornhuskers were the Associated Press defending national champions, Coach Bob Devaney had downplayed their chance of repeating, calling it a "a real shot in the dark." Only five programs had won back-to-back national titles since the AP rankings were established in 1936. Even so, Nebraska wouldn't "abdicate" its position as Big Eight and national champion without a fight, he said.

Coach Chuck Fairbanks's Oklahoma team had the more surprising record, having gone 7–4–1 the previous season, during which assistant Barry Switzer had persuaded Fairbanks to change his offense to a Wishbone attack—popularized by bitter rival Texas—three games in. Any lingering questions were erased in October, when Oklahoma defeated national contenders Southern California (33–20), Texas (48–27), and Colorado (45–17) on consecutive Saturdays, then punctuated the streak by overwhelming Kansas State, 75–28.

Nebraska was no less impressive, shutting out three of its first five Big Eight opponents. After the third of those shutouts against Iowa State, Cyclone quarterback Dean Carlson said the only defense in the country comparable to Nebraska's had to be that of the NFL's Minnesota Vikings.

The Associated Press all-conference team, announced the week of the game, included nine Cornhuskers and eight Sooners among the twenty-two first-team selections. In addition, Nebraska defensive tackle Larry Jacobson was named the Outland Trophy winner. A year later, that award would go to Rich Glover, who played alongside Jacobson at

Barry Switzer (left) and Tom Osborne were the offensive coordinators in the Game of the Century. Both became the head coaches at their respective schools in 1973. (Courtesy Huskers Illustrated*)*

middle guard. Glover also would be voted the Lombardi Award, giving Nebraska a sweep of major awards in 1972, with wingback Johnny Rodgers winning the Heisman Trophy.

Oklahoma's Pruitt finished second in the Heisman voting in 1972, after finishing third in 1971, behind Auburn's Pat Sullivan and Cornell's Ed Marinaro. The announcement that Sullivan had won the trophy came during halftime of the nationally televised Georgia–Georgia Tech game Thanksgiving night. Sullivan might not have been the best collegiate quarterback, however, according to *Sports Illustrated*'s Dan Jenkins. That distinction might have belonged to Nebraska's Jerry Tagge and Oklahoma's Jack Mildren; take your pick. They certainly were the "most complete," Jenkins wrote before the game.

Mildren, a junior, was more runner than passer—he didn't complete a pass against USC—and Tagge, a senior, was more passer than runner, though he was strong and not averse to tucking away the ball and running if the situation demanded. Tagge was among four high school teammates from Green Bay, Wisconsin, whom Nebraska had recruited, and two of the others also were starters in 1970 and 1971, cornerback Jim Anderson and monster back Dave Mason. Anderson and Tagge were team captains in 1971.

That Nebraska was able to get Tagge away from Wisconsin and Michigan State was easier than it might have appeared. He was born in Omaha, though his father was in the Air Force and was transferred from the Strategic Air Command base in Bellevue, Nebraska, to Green Bay when Tagge was four years old. His dad, who grew up in Wood River, Nebraska, accompanied him on a recruiting visit to Nebraska and was allowed to kick back in Devaney's office chair and wear one of Devaney's distinctive red hats.

Tagge was slowed by injuries and didn't play much on the freshman team. He alternated with Van Brownson as a sophomore and to a lesser degree as a junior, taking over as the season went on. He scored the winning touchdown against LSU in the 1971 Orange Bowl game, stretching the ball across the goal line to give Nebraska its first national championship. Osborne, who met regularly with the quarterbacks, played an important role in his development. "Nobody thought I could play except Tom," Tagge said.

Nebraska's offense was built around him, Rodgers, and senior I-back Jeff Kinney, who had been recruited out of high school in McCook, Nebraska, as a quarterback. Every Big Eight school except Oklahoma had shown an interest in Kinney, whose father was a brakeman for the Burlington Northern Railroad. But he was leaning toward accepting the Cornhuskers' scholarship offer before his senior year in high school, following a visit from Osborne. Even so, coaches from Texas, UCLA, and Tennessee also traveled to McCook and tried to persuade him to leave the state. When Devaney came to town to pick up his signed letter of intent, "it was like entertaining the president of the United States," he said.

Kinney was moved to flanker as a freshman, leading the freshman team in receptions, and then to halfback in Nebraska's evolving offense. He led the varsity in rushing, receiving, and scoring in 1969, to earn conference sophomore-of-the-year honors. His play was the most impressive by a Cornhusker sophomore since that of All-America Bobby Reynolds in 1950, according to the media guide. Learning to play I-back that first varsity season wasn't easy. "At the time, I thought I was a better receiver than runner," said Kinney. "I wasn't a great runner because I couldn't read blocks very well. I just had to learn how to run to daylight. The last two or three games I started coming around."

His opportunity as a sophomore had come, in part, because of a season-ending injury to Joe Orduna, who returned in 1970, when the two alternated. Replacing Orduna was among the most significant concerns going into 1971, according to Devaney. But he needn't have worried. Kinney carried the load and became the second player in school history to rush for 1,000 yards — Reynolds was the first. Kinney was among six Cornhuskers who earned All-America recognition in 1971. He was included on the *Time* magazine team. Tagge, Rodgers, Jacobson, Glover, and defensive end Willie Harper were the others, with the last four being consensus selections. Harper, like Rodgers and Glover, was a junior.

Mildren, Pruitt, and junior center Tom Brahaney were Oklahoma's All-Americans in 1971. The battle involving Brahaney and Glover was a key to the game. Glover went a long way toward winning the Outland Trophy and Lombardi Award a year later that day, making twenty-two tackles. "I don't want to say he played like a madman because he was controlled," said Nebraska's Al Austin. "But he just . . . had an instinct for where the ball was going. He went right through double teams, I don't know how many times."

Austin was a story himself. The sophomore from Lincoln had been a backup but was put into the starting lineup in place of senior Carl Johnson, a first-team all-conference right tackle. Johnson had suffered a knee strain against Kansas State twelve days before, and though he was able to practice the week of the game, Devaney had decided to go with Austin and see if he could hold up against Sooner all-conference defensive end Raymond Hamilton. Despite giving up experience, Austin held his own.

Jeff Kinney (35) hits a hole being cleared by All-America tackle Bob Newton (74), on the road to Nebraska's first national championship in a game against Kansas in 1970. (Courtesy UNL Photography)

There were as many other stories as there were players. The game was special for Nebraska defensive tackle Bill Janssen because his older brother, Carl, an Air Force pilot in Vietnam, was on leave and in the stands, watching him play as a collegian for the first time. Carl had played football at the Air Force Academy, and when the game was over, he hustled onto the field and tackled Bill in celebration.

Cornhusker senior Bill Kosch, a two-time, first-team all-conference safety, was moved to cornerback for the game as the defensive coaches tried to account for Jon Harrison, a 5'9", 157-pound split end and Mildren's high school teammate. The plan was to put Kosch on Harrison in man-to-man coverage instead of the zone coverage to which he was accustomed and use cornerback Joe Blahak at safety. Blahak was the better tackler and could help against the run. He forced one of Oklahoma's three lost fumbles and recovered another, but covering the speedy Harrison would be a nightmare for Kosch.

The anticipation—Carly Simon's gold album by that name, *Anticipation*, was released three days before the game—was such that more than 500 press credentials were issued, and ticket scalpers did a brisk business. The *New York Times* reported that a pair of $6.00 tickets on the 45-yard line went for $100.00, prompting the Oklahoma student newspaper to contact the Internal Revenue Service office in Oklahoma City to inquire whether the scalpers were violating federal wage-price stabilization guidelines. The announced attendance of 61,826 was an Owen Field record, and the television audience was estimated at between fifty-five million and eighty million, the largest ever to watch a college football game. (An Admiral color television set, console model, could be purchased in Lincoln for $197 plus trade-in.)

Owen Field was a horseshoe, the south end open except for low bleachers. The temperature at kickoff was forty-nine degrees, and the wind—regarded as more of a

Best of the Best

Coach Bob Devaney's 1971 Nebraska team is rated among the best in college football history, as is Coach Tom Osborne's 1995 team. Both were dominant in going undefeated, after also winning national championships the previous season.

1971 (13–0)
Sept. 11 Oregon 34–7
Sept. 18 Minnesota 35–7
Sept. 25 Texas A&M 34–7
Oct. 2 Utah State 42–6
Oct. 9 at Missouri 36–0
Oct. 16 Kansas 55–0
Oct. 23 at Oklahoma State 41–13
Oct. 30 Colorado 31–7
Nov. 6 Iowa State 37–0
Nov. 13 at Kansas State 44–17
Nov. 25 at Oklahoma 35–31
Dec. 4 at Hawaii 45–3
Jan. 1 Alabama (Orange Bowl) 38–6

1995 (12–0)
Aug. 31 at Oklahoma State 64–21
Sept. 9 at Michigan State 50–10
Sept. 16 Arizona State 77–28
Sept. 23 Pacific 49–7
Sept. 30 Washington State 35–21
Oct. 14 Missouri 57–0
Oct. 21 Kansas State 49–25
Oct. 28 at Colorado 44–21
Nov. 4 Iowa State 73–14
Nov. 11 at Kansas 41–3
Nov. 24 Oklahoma 37–0
Jan. 2 Florida (Fiesta Bowl) 62–24

factor for Nebraska because of its passing—was from the south at from sixteen to twenty-three miles per hour. The sky was overcast, with little prospect of sunshine, "not even when Bob Devaney walks on the field, I fear," said Nebraska radio broadcast legend Lyell Bremser.

Nebraska scored first, less than four minutes into the game, when Oklahoma was forced to punt after three runs gained 5 yards. Rodgers fielded Joe Wylie's 34-yard kick at the Cornhusker 28 yard line and returned it 72 yards for a touchdown. Pruitt, who wore a T-shirt that said "Hello" on the front and "Goodbye" on the back beneath his pads, could have stopped Rodgers before he got started but couldn't hold on. Sooner lineman Ken Jones, who, like Rodgers, was from Omaha, also had a shot at a tackle. The return by Rodgers was set up to the right, but he saw an opportunity to the left and that's where he headed. Clete Fischer, who coached the kick return team, "gave me the green light to do whatever I wanted to do after a [sophomore] year of successfully doing it," Rodgers said years later. "I wasn't into that visualization stuff, but I could imagine I was going to score . . . the script was, there was no script."

In retrospect, given how close Pruitt was, "I probably should have made a fair catch," said Rodgers. But he tried to return everything he could get to and catch. He had already returned punts for touchdowns against Oklahoma State (92 yards) and Iowa State (62 yards) that season, and he would return another against Alabama (77 yards) in the Orange Bowl game to wrap up the national championship. He also returned a kickoff 98 yards for a touchdown against Texas A&M. "As great as that team was, take Johnny Rodgers out of there on kickoff and punt returns and it probably wouldn't have gone 13–0," Osborne said.

Rodgers got some help along the way, including at least two blocks that might have been ruled clips, the first by John Adkins on Wylie and the second by Blahak on Harrison, the last Sooner with any hope of catching Rodgers. Blahak's block has attracted the most attention over the years. "It's gotten to the point where I say, 'Did the referee throw a flag? Then it wasn't a clip,' " said Blahak. Had he made the tackle as he should have, Pruitt said, the issue of a clip would have been moot.

Oklahoma responded with a 30-yard John Carroll field goal, set up by a 32-yard pass play from Mildren to Harrison on a third and 8. Late in the first quarter, Nebraska had

National Championship Material

The "Game of the Century" included three assistant coaches who would go on to lead teams to national championships as college head coaches. In addition to Nebraska's Tom Osborne, who would coach the Cornhuskers to national championships in 1994, 1995, and 1997, Oklahoma assistants included Barry Switzer and Jimmy Johnson, who coached four national championship teams between them; Switzer had three at Oklahoma (1974, 1975, 1985) and Johnson one (1987) at Miami.

Johnson also coached the Dallas Cowboys to two Super Bowl titles and Switzer coached them to one, while Devaney assistant Monte Kiffin would be the defensive coordinator for the Tampa Bay Buccaneers Super Bowl champions, after being a head coach at the college level.

crossed midfield on a drive to take the lead after Blahak forced a Pruitt fumble and Anderson recovered at his own 46 yard line. The Wishbone was a high-risk offense because of the ball handling it required, and the Sooners had lost an average of nearly three fumbles per game. The consensus was, if they could avoid turnovers, they would be difficult to beat. They would lose two more critical fumbles before the afternoon was over.

Nebraska needed twelve plays, ten of them runs, to increase its lead to 14–3 on the first of Kinney's four touchdowns and a Rich Sanger extra-point kick. Cornhusker fans breathed a little easier. Their team had not been behind in a game all season. By halftime, however, Nebraska would trail 17–14.

Despite losing a fumble at the Nebraska 27 yard line, Oklahoma scored two touchdowns near the end of the second quarter, largely through Mildren's efforts. He scored

Congratulations

President Richard Nixon spent thirty minutes after the "Game of the Century" trying to get through to the Nebraska locker room by telephone to congratulate Bob Devaney and his team. The Cornhusker coach reportedly told the president, "They sold a lot of popcorn today. Nobody left." Nixon was no stranger to Cornhusker football. He had come to Lincoln to present the 1970 Associated Press national championship trophy to Devaney and captains Dan Schneiss and Jerry Murtaugh at a packed NU Coliseum.

the first on a 2-yard run, finishing a 13-play, 80-yard drive on which he gained nearly half the yards, then passed to Harrison for the second, a play that covered 24 yards and stunned Nebraska. Oklahoma's final series of the half had begun at its own 22 yard line, with 33 seconds remaining. After 2 running plays gained 11 yards, Mildren and Harrison teamed up on a 43-yard pass play with 16 seconds remaining. The next play was the touchdown pass.

Oklahoma had dominated the statistics to that point, with 310 total yards and 14 first downs to Nebraska's 91 total yards and 5 first downs. "I felt bad at halftime," Glover recalled later. But Devaney remained upbeat, encouraging his players, telling them they had no reason to hang their heads.

Nebraska's offense came out for the second half determined to be physical and run right at the Sooners, an approach reflected on the first play from scrimmage when Kinney broke a tackle and muscled his way for a 22-yard gain. The Cornhuskers regained the lead 6 minutes later on Kinney's 3-yard touchdown run, after Mildren lost a fumble near midfield. The big play in the abbreviated drive was a 32-yard run by Tagge on third and 3 at the Oklahoma 35 yard line. The play was an option with fullback Bill Olds to the right, out of a spread formation. Tagge faked a pitch and turned up the field.

Less than two minutes later, Nebraska had the ball back, covering 61 yards in 8 plays, one a 10-yard, Tagge-to-Rodgers pass to the Oklahoma 1 yard line. From there Kinney scored again. With 3:38 remaining in the third quarter, the Cornhuskers appeared to be back in control, at 28–17. But that appearance was quickly shattered, again through the efforts of Mildren and some trickery involving

Harrison, who completed a pass to tight end Al Chandler for a 51-yard gain. Mildren gained the other 22 yards in the 7-play series, the last 3 for a touchdown with 28 seconds left in the quarter. Then Oklahoma took back the lead with 7:10 remaining in the game, when Mildren passed to Harrison for 16 yards and a touchdown on a fourth and 5. Carroll's extra point made the score 31–28.

After the game, Devaney would tell the *Lincoln Journal and Star* that he wasn't concerned about being behind for the second time. "I figured we could score," he said. "I was worried that we might score too quickly and give them a chance to come back."

What followed was a dramatic drive that defined Devaney's next-to-last team as one of college football's best. The Cornhuskers covered 74 yards on 12 plays, 7 of them carries by Kinney and one a pass from Tagge to Rodgers for an 11-yard gain to keep the drive alive. Rodgers' punt return to initiate the scoring has come to characterize the game, but his third-down catch at the Oklahoma 35 yard line with 4:37 remaining was the critical play. Nebraska faced third and 8.

Rodgers was supposed to go 15 yards but adjusted his route when he saw Tagge under pressure from the Sooners' Hamilton, who had gotten past Austin for one of the few times in the game. That was his "worst mistake of the day," Austin recalled. Tagge was able to get outside of Hamilton, however, and find Rodgers, splitting two linebackers with a throw that Rodgers had to go down to get. Given the situation, Tagge said, he had no choice but to throw the pass low. "I don't think, 'You gotta catch this one or we'll be in trouble.' Instead, I just figure I'll get it," Rodgers told the *Lincoln Journal and Star* afterward. "I saw Jerry was in

Johnny Rodgers (right) couldn't hold everything he got his hands on, but it seemed that way to opponents. (Courtesy UNL Photography)

Welcome Back

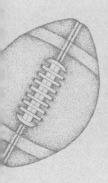

A crowd estimated at between 30,000 and 32,000 packed the grounds at the Lincoln Municipal Airport to welcome back the team from Oklahoma. People were lined ten deep along the fences and enough got past to force the team to unload on the runway instead of at the terminal. Traffic was so heavy on the roads leading to the airport that Lincoln police finally began stopping cars, according to the *Lincoln Star.*

trouble, so I glanced over to see where the first-down marker was and started cutting across the field at that point."

Nebraska wouldn't face another third down until the play on which Kinney scored, following the lead of fullback Maury Damkroger off a block by tackle Daryl White and into the pages of Cornhusker history, his white tear-away jersey so tattered that the number 35 could no longer be read.

Oklahoma still had 1:33 to respond. But the Sooners had to start at their own 19 yard line, and after a Mildren pass sailed over the head of Harrison, who was running open near midfield, Nebraska's defense put the final touches on the victory. Mildren kept for 4 yards. Jacobson sacked him for an 8-yard loss, and then on fourth down, he applied more pressure, with Glover batting down a desperation pass.

After four Nebraska running plays and two Oklahoma timeouts, the final 1:10 on the clock elapsed. "You never lose a game; time just runs out," Janssen said years later. His respect for the Sooners was typical. Even in defeat, Mildren "was probably the player of the game," said Tagge. Mildren rushed for 130 yards and 2 touchdowns on 31 carries and completed 5 of 10 passes for 137 yards and the 2 touchdowns to Harrison. He might not have been impressive as a passer going into the game but "he looked like Johnny Unitas out there today," Devaney told reporters.

Kinney, who went to the sideline briefly during the winning drive because his legs were cramping, finished with 174 rushing yards and the 4 touchdowns. He gained 154 of the yards in the second half. "If we hadn't won, the whole season—in fact, my whole career—would have seemed for naught," he told the Lincoln newspapers.

The game's significance is diminished with the passing years. Each season has its outstanding teams, and those who make the judgments become younger, with grainy film and written words as their only links to Thanksgiving Day of 1971, when Nebraska and Oklahoma played. But "I think that was the game of the century, from my standpoint," said Janssen, "what was on the table, the character, the players, the tradition of the program. At the time you didn't have any inkling that this was going to be as important as it was. It hits me on occasion, and I'm very, very thankful to have been part of it."

Most who were involved that day, on both sides, have said the same thing.

For Love of the Game

On the first day of the fall semester classes in 1997, Nebraska coach Tom Osborne called Jason Schwab over before practice. "Hey, Schwabbie," he said, "I need to see you after practice." Schwab, a sophomore walk-on offensive tackle, wondered what he had done to warrant such a meeting. "I thought, 'What in the hell did I do now?'" he would say later. Concern about some forgotten wrongdoing nagged him throughout a mistake-prone practice, and it was with understandable trepidation that he approached Osborne afterward. "We're going to give you a scholarship," Osborne told him.

Schwab tried to mask his elation, compounded by a sense of relief, acting as if he had expected to earn a scholarship from the day he arrived on campus, unwanted, as he saw it, by any other NCAA Division I-A program. Even North Dakota State, a Division II school, had turned him down for a scholarship because, the coach said, he wasn't explosive enough. Such an assessment might have been based on limited information. Schwab missed most of his senior season at Cretin-Derham High School in Saint Paul, Minnesota, because of a hyperextended knee. But whatever the reason, he realized he would have to pay his own way if he wanted to play at the major college level.

Coach Tom Osborne and the captains of the 1995 national championship team: Christian Peter, Aaron Graham, Phil Ellis, and Jared Tomich, a two-time All-American who came to Nebraska as a walk-on. (Courtesy Huskers Illustrated)

And he would have to find a program willing to let him do even that.

As it turned out, Nebraska was willing, after watching some videotape. Schwab was so pleased that he got a tattoo on his left biceps during his freshman year, the Cornhuskers' block N with "O-line" across it. When his mom saw the tattoo, "she cried for days," said Schwab. If he hadn't succeeded, it would have been an indelible reminder of a dream not realized. But he overcame two major surgeries during six years—the NCAA granted an additional season of eligibility—to earn the scholarship and start as a junior and senior, when he was elected as a cocaptain.

Schwab's story was commonplace at Nebraska under Osborne. It became a haven for walk-on players. Typically, they came from high schools in the state, but some sought out the Cornhuskers from considerable distance, including Isaiah Hipp, once known as college football's most famous walk-on. Most programs can recount walk-on success stories. But Nebraska was unique in encouraging athletes who, for reasons of height, weight, strength, or speed, were overlooked by recruiters offering scholarships. In the late 1970s and early 1980s in particular, walk-ons and Nebraska were synonymous. "Walk-ons have been the salvation of our program," Osborne once said.

At its height the Cornhusker walk-on program included as many as eighty hopefuls, who would play on the junior varsity team as freshmen, sit out a redshirt season, and then contribute, if not on the top offensive and defensive units or on special teams then at least on the scout squad during practice. Nebraska was able to conduct more practice stations than most programs because of its walk-ons. As a result "you got to rep the hell out of plays," said Bill Lewis, an All-American at center in 1985. Lewis, who played seven NFL seasons, was a scholarship recruit but respected the contributions of walk-ons. Multiple practice stations were "absolutely essential to Nebraska's success," he said. "I don't know if another program in the country had that. There was nothing close in the NFL."

Nebraska's strength and conditioning program was essential in developing walk-ons. Schwab weighed 290 pounds with 20 percent body fat when he arrived as a freshman. A two-time finalist for the team's Lifter of the Year Award, he weighed 305 with 13 percent body fat as a senior.

Keys to Success

Like Langston Coleman, brothers Jimmy and Toby Williams walked on at Nebraska after outstanding high school athletic careers in Washington, D.C. Jimmy Williams, a defensive end, was a cocaptain as a senior in 1981 and earned first-team All-America recognition. Other walk-ons who have been first-team All-Americans include defensive end Derrie Nelson (1980), I-back Jarvis Redwine (1980), rush end Jared Tomich (1995–96), and punter Kyle Larson (2003).

The Williams brothers walked on at Nebraska, they told the *Lincoln Sunday Journal and Star,* not only because they had watched the Cornhuskers' annual game against Oklahoma on television, but also because they had heard about I. M. Hipp, who gained national attention as a walk-on. Hipp, a junior when they arrived, was an inspiration to them, Jimmy Williams told the *Sunday Journal and Star.* "We saw him work harder than anybody we've ever seen," said Williams. "We figured if that's what it took to make it, that's what we were both going to give."

During the summer before Jimmy's senior season—Toby was a junior because of a redshirt—the two of them rose at 4:30 A.M. five days a week and walked 2 miles to work. After work, they went to the stadium and spent two and a half hours in the weight room before returning home in the evening.

"All we want is what Isaiah had," Jimmy said, explaining their commitment. "He's the only guy we know who had his personal set of keys to the weight room."

Walk-ons were less common under Bob Devaney, Osborne's Hall of Fame predecessor, because scholarships were considerably more abundant. In the early 1970s, however, the NCAA began reducing the number of scholarships that programs could award, now twenty-five per year with a maximum of eighty-five for a team. The number of walk-ons has been reduced as well, in part because of an increasing number of Division I-A programs that offer scholarships to players who might have walked on otherwise. In addition there has been talk of limiting rosters to 105 as a cost-cutting measure. That would mean a program with all of its scholarships filled could have no more than twenty walk-ons.

Nebraska's walk-ons are now recruited. Like scholarship athletes, they make campus visits and provide videotape to be evaluated. Those who show up for a tryout sight unseen, the way former Cornhusker defensive end Langston Coleman did in 1963, are rare if nonexistent.

Coleman came to Nebraska from Western High in Washington, D.C., where he was an all-metro selection and earned letters in basketball, baseball, and swimming, as well as in football. He had opportunities to go to other schools, but he was persuaded to contact Nebraska. His mom worked in the office of Ted Sorensen, a Nebraska native and University of Nebraska alum who had been a speech writer for President John F. Kennedy. Coleman was a high school senior when Devaney went to Nebraska from Wyoming, and Sorensen asked if he might consider playing for the Cornhuskers. "Sure," said Coleman, who then wrote a letter to Devaney.

Devaney wrote back. "No one wrote the kind of letters Coach Devaney wrote," Coleman once told the *Sunday*

Journal and Star. So at summer's end, he packed up and hitchhiked to Nebraska, along with a friend. "We didn't know much about either one of them," Devaney said years later. His friend didn't play for the Cornhuskers, but Coleman quickly established himself with his athletic ability and aggressiveness, setting a standard for those who followed. "During practice, the other players used to hate being in drills with Langston because he'd beat the heck out of guys," said Devaney. "He was one of the meanest football players we ever had at Nebraska."

On-field nastiness was a way to get noticed in the midst of all those scholarship players. Anonymity is the companion of most freshmen, whether on scholarship or as walk-ons. One day in the fall of 1995, while working on the scout team, Schwab inadvertently fell into the knees of cocaptain and defensive tackle Christian Peter, who "thought I was trying to take him out," Schwab recalled. In an instant Schwab was at the bottom of a pile of defenders, wondering where he was and how he had gotten there, whether he might have been run over by a bus. When the defenders got up, "you're laying by yourself and the drill has moved down 20 yards," he said. The coaches "don't have time to deal with that kind of stuff, so you just lay by yourself for a while, until you come to."

College Football's Most Famous Walk-On

Nebraska didn't spend much on the recruitment of Isaiah Moses Walter Hipp, about 13 cents, the price of a postage stamp in the mid-1970s. Hipp made the initial contact. South Carolina wasn't in the Cornhuskers' recruiting area. And when he did, they sent him a questionnaire in reply.

Financial Frustrations

Technically, walk-ons cease to be walk-ons when they climb to the top of the depth chart because then they are put on scholarship. Under Coach Tom Osborne, Nebraska held back scholarships from its NCAA limit of eighty-five to reward walk-ons. But getting a scholarship didn't always mean an end to the financial frustrations.

Aaron Terpening, a rover and special teams player, came to Nebraska from Salem, Oregon, drawn by a youthful interest in the Cornhuskers that came about because his dad had once lived in Lincoln. Terpening was put on scholarship in the spring of his third year, with the understanding that it would be only for a semester. In the fall of his junior year, he was paying his own way again. "Those are the times it really takes patience and trust to know that things will work out," he said. "Of course it's disappointing and a bit frustrating." He went back on scholarship for his senior season, 2002, after earning a starting position.

Hipp, a running back, responded with an impressive resume. He had sprinter's speed, having run the 100-yard dash in 9.9 seconds. And he had rushed for nearly 3,000 yards during his high school career, averaging more than 5 yards per carry and earning prep All-America recognition despite missing five games during his senior season because of a collarbone injury.

But the town in which he lived, tiny Chapin, South Carolina, was off the beaten path. His great-grandmother helped raise him and his sister in a three-room cabin, following the separation of their parents. And the major college programs that had shown an interest in him before the broken collarbone, among them Oklahoma, UCLA, Texas, Texas A&M, and Florida, had stopped calling. Had South Carolina offered a scholarship, he would have accepted readily, he once said. But it wasn't interested either, despite its proximity, and he decided that if he were going to pay his own way somewhere, he would leave the area, escape the racial attitudes with which he had grown up.

His interest in Nebraska was based in part on having watched on television as the Cornhuskers defeated Bear Bryant's Alabama team 38–6 in the 1972 Orange Bowl game, earning a second consecutive national championship. Hipp was fifteen years old at the time, an impressionable age.

Nebraska's willingness to allow him to walk on created other problems, among them how to get to Lincoln. Hipp, who had never been farther west than Atlanta and had never flown, had to borrow $96 from a girlfriend for airfare. And once he got to Lincoln, he had to pay his own way, which he did with a federal grant, available because the Cornhuskers hadn't recruited him. Had Nebraska recruited him, even though he walked on, he wouldn't have been eligible for the Basic Educational Opportunity Grant money.

NCAA rules allowed schools to award maximums of thirty football scholarships per year and ninety-five total, and the Cornhuskers had used their allotted thirty. One went to quarterback Vince Ferragamo, a transfer from California, and two went to junior college transfers. The remaining twenty-seven went to high school seniors, including five who were listed as running backs, Hipp's position.

*"College football's most famous walk-on," I. M. Hipp
(Courtesy UNL Photography)*

The most prominent of the five was 6'2", 200-pound Richard Berns from Wichita Falls, Texas. Berns, who had run the 100 in 9.7 seconds, was heavily recruited by Oklahoma and Texas, among others, and was regarded as a blue chip prospect, although "I don't like the description of a boy as a 'Blue-Chipper,' " Nebraska Coach Tom Osborne told the *Sunday Journal and Star*. The reason, Osborne said, was that "some players come with all the credentials in the world yet never develop. Others blossom late." Whatever the designation, Hipp faced long odds when he reported for freshman practice, a fact underscored by Jim Ross, the Cornhusker freshman coach.

"What position do you play?" Ross asked.

"I-back," Hipp replied.

"We'll see," Ross said.

As it turned out, Ross liked what he saw. Hipp would alternate with Berns and lead a 5–0 freshman team in rushing with 366 yards and 4 touchdowns on 67 carries. But success on the freshman team didn't necessarily mean success on the varsity. Walter Wallace, a walk-on who played high school football on a military base in Aviano, Italy, led the Cornhusker freshman team in rushing in 1978, with 561 yards and 7 touchdowns in 5 games, but never played a down for the varsity. And the same was true of Will Curtis, a walk-on from Baltimore who was the freshman team's leading rusher in 1981.

In any case Hipp sat out his second season as a redshirt while Berns played, beginning preseason practice at number four on the depth chart and working his way to the top. He broke the school single-game rushing record with 211 yards against Hawaii in the final game of the regular season.

Though he didn't play in games, Hipp made the most of that second year at Nebraska, developing a reputation in the weight room that would include winning the team's Lifter of the Year Award twice. He was so dedicated, in fact, that he had his own keys to the weight room. He set team position records in the bench press and power clean as well as a weight class record on the hip sled.

Berns was the clear-cut starter at I-back going into preseason practice in 1977, with senior Monte Anthony second on the depth chart, and Hipp, still without a scholarship, third. However, injury problems continued to plague Anthony, as they had done the previous season, plus he was spending time at fullback as well as at I-back, thereby increasing Hipp's chances of getting on the field. Mike Corgan regularly rotated I-backs, so that a backup in whom he had confidence could expect to see action.

Corgan, who coached "the business" of running back with a stern demeanor, arms crossed, and an omnipresent pipe with which he punctuated his words, emphasized the need to go into contact when it couldn't be avoided, and Hipp was a prize student of Iron Mike's system. Corgan's confidence in Hipp was tested in the opening game of 1977 against Washington State. When Berns had to go to the sideline to replace a torn tear-away jersey, Hipp got his first varsity carry and fumbled the ball away at the Washington State 2 yard line. He wouldn't carry again until the next week, during a regionally televised 31–24 upset of fourth-ranked Alabama. He rushed for 38 yards on 6 carries and caught a pass for a 53-yard gain, complementing Berns, whom *Sports Illustrated* selected as its national offensive player of the week. Going back to the previous season, Berns had rushed for 100 or more yards in 4 consecutive games.

But a hip pointer in the first quarter of the third game of the 1977 season did what opposing defenses hadn't been able to do—slowed Berns down. He went to the sideline and watched as Hipp rushed for 122 yards and a touchdown in a 31–10 victory against Baylor, setting the stage for back-to-back performances that would earn Hipp a place in the pages of *Sports Illustrated* and lead Nebraska sports information director Don Bryant to describe him as "college football's most famous walk-on."

With Berns ailing Hipp started for the first time against Indiana—the Cornhuskers' fourth and final nonconference game, all at Memorial Stadium—and rushed for 254 yards, averaging nearly 10 yards per carry. The yardage was a school single-game record, breaking the previous mark, Berns's 211 against Hawaii, and it was the most by any major college running back that season. At Kansas State the next week, in a 26–9 victory that solidified Nebraska's claim to a number nine ranking in the Associated Press poll, Hipp rushed for 207 yards and 2 touchdowns—on runs of 66 yards and a school-record 82 yards.

Hipp was the talk of the college football world, mentioned in the same breath with Heisman Trophy candidate running backs Earl Campbell of Texas and Terry Miller of Oklahoma State. He had the numbers to go with a name that was a headline writer's dream: "I'm Hipp," "Hipp, Hipp, Hooray." The imaginative Bryant referred to him as "Hoppity Hipp," an allusion to Husker history. Harry Hopp, a back on the 1941 Rose Bowl team, carried the nickname "Hippity Hopp."

Hipp was named Isaiah Moses at birth. His mom called him Ike. He added Walter when he was sixteen, at the urging of his father, Walter, a bishop in the Kingdom of

God Church. Boyd Epley, Nebraska's strength and conditioning coach, was the first to call him by his initials, I. M., he would recall later, and Corgan, who knew the initials stood for biblical names, called him "Zeke," as in "Ezekiel." Being identified by his initials had symbolic significance for Hipp, who had grown up imagining himself as another O. J. Simpson. And like Simpson, he wore a number 32 jersey.

Hipp enjoyed the attention. Might he win three Heisman Trophies, he was asked. "That's just a big dream," he was quoted in a Lincoln newspaper. "I guess everyone has to have some dreams." And those dreams seemed realistic. He rushed for 165 yards in his third start against Iowa State and 172 yards in his fourth against Colorado, despite battling the flu and losing eleven pounds the week of the game.

In just 5 games, he had rushed for nearly 1,000 yards and 8 touchdowns. His run of games in which he rushed for 100 or more yards ended there, however, and he would reach that total only once more during his sophomore season, gaining 200 against Kansas. Even so, his 1,301 rushing yards for the season were the second most in Cornhusker history. Bobby Reynolds set the record, also as a sophomore, running for 1,342 yards in only nine games in 1950. Nebraska had only two other 1,000-yard rushers at the time, Jeff Kinney in 1971 and Tony Davis in 1973.

As with Reynolds, Hipp's finest season was his first. He was selected to the All-Big Eight first team, a consensus pick, and the United Press International All-America second team. Given his sophomore success, Hipp predicted that he would rush for 2,000 yards in 1978. No NCAA Division I player had ever rushed for 2,000 yards in a season. Pittsburgh's Tony Dorsett had come close in 1976, gaining 1,948

Long Walk

The majority of Nebraska's walk-ons have come from in-state high schools. But the program also has attracted players from coast to coast—and beyond. Among those who earned letters were Canadians Peter Buchanan (1988) and Terris Chorney (1990–92). Buchanan, a linebacker, was from Pierre Fonds, Quebec. Chorney, a center, was from Ituna, Saskatchewan. Brett Popplewell, a two-year letterman (1992–93) at wide receiver, was from Melbourne, Australia, where he played American football as well as Australian Rules football at Carey Grammar Prep School.

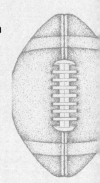

yards. Southern California's Marcus Allen would be the first to do it, two seasons after Hipp finished at Nebraska, gaining 2,342 yards on a record 403 carries. Two years after that, Heisman Trophy winner Mike Rozier would become the first 2,000-yard rusher for the Cornhuskers.

Hipp managed just half that, counting 66 yards in the Orange Bowl game—though at the time, official NCAA statistics didn't include bowl games. So his official total was 936 yards. "I don't know how the 2,000-yard thing came about, whether he was prodded or what," a displeased Corgan said prior to the 1979 season. "It makes good copy for the newspapers, but using two I-backs the way we do, that's an impossibility. Isaiah had his sights pretty high, and now he's more realistic." Or at least more reserved. Hipp said he intended to keep personal goals to himself.

His senior season was frustrating, in part because of a nagging turf toe injury that might have had something to do

Jarvis Redwine paid his own way in transferring from Oregon State to earn All-America recognition and the nickname "Marvelous Jarvis." (Courtesy UNL Photography)

with his wearing size 8½ shoes, even though his feet were size 10. The smaller shoes and resultant tight fit helped him to avoid slipping and sliding, he said. The shoes were among of a handful of idiosyncrasies, which included wearing thermal undershirts beneath his shoulder pads. Glen Abbott, the Cornhuskers' equipment manager, kept a half-dozen of the shirts on hand, with sleeves clipped and number 32 written with a black laundry marker on the backs. A man back home known as "Uncle Jim" had worn such shirts, Hipp said. They kept him cool.

Hipp trimmed down for his final season, losing the ten pounds he had gained to deal with the physical punishment he expected following his breakout performance in 1977. In retrospect the additional weight had been a mistake, he said. He was constantly off balance, as if "I was stumbling all the time." He rushed for 167 yards in the opener. By the fourth game, however, he had lost the starting job. He would finish as the Cornhuskers' career-rushing leader, surpassing Berns, but he would do so in relative anonymity. By the end of the 1979 season, attention had turned to his successor at I-back, Jarvis Redwine, a walk-on transfer from Inglewood, California, by way of Oregon State, where he had played as a freshman. Redwine would make the cover of *Sports Illustrated* and be known as "Marvelous Jarvis."

The Turning Point

B ob Devaney was partial to passing during his time as Duffy Daugherty's assistant at Michigan State. That's how Daugherty remembered it. Devaney, who played end on offense and linebacker on defense at Alma College, would suggest the Spartans throw more, Daugherty said, and he would decline. Passing was fine, he told his assistant, but running led to success.

After Devaney became the head coach at Wyoming, Daugherty would check the statistics each week and see that the Cowboys were running, rarely passing, and winning, while his Spartans were passing, rarely running, and losing. That fact wasn't lost on Devaney, who called one day to ask what he thought he was doing. The Spartans were passing, Daugherty replied, because they couldn't run.

Daugherty and Devaney were both great storytellers, but typically, there was truth embedded in their stories. Devaney brought a run-oriented offense to Nebraska, with two of his first four Cornhusker teams leading the nation in rushing and the other two ranking in the top ten. They operated from a T formation, with a full-house backfield and an unbalanced line, and were a combined 45–5, winning four consecutive Big Eight championships in Devaney's first five seasons.

The need for change was apparent after 6–4 records in 1967 and 1968, however, and Devaney gave Tom Osborne, his receivers coach, the responsibility for redesigning the offense. Devaney wanted an I-formation attack, which

Running Men

Under Coach Tom Osborne, Nebraska developed college football's most dominating running offense. From 1980 through 1997, when he stepped aside, the Cornhuskers led the nation in rushing eleven times. From 1978 through 1997, they never ranked lower than fourth nationally in rushing. Also during those seasons, Nebraska led the nation in total offense three times and finished second five times.

The Cornhuskers had outstanding I-backs, among them I. M. Hipp, Jarvis Redwine, Roger Craig, Mike Rozier, Doug DuBose, Keith Jones, Ken Clark, Derek Brown, Calvin Jones, Lawrence Phillips and Ahman Green. And their quarterbacks were like additional running backs. The goal was "not necessarily to recruit sprinters at quarterback but speed," Osborne said. "If a guy could pass on top of that, it was a plus. But we wanted to make sure he could run."

Besides Turner Gill, Steve Taylor, and Tommie Frazier, who led the Cornhuskers to national championships in 1994 and 1995, the list of quarterbacks who could run included Gerry Gdowski and Scott Frost, who transferred from Stanford to direct the 1997 national championship team.

provided more offensive production and balance between run and pass.

Osborne, like Devaney when he was Daugherty's assistant, was originally a "passing guy," offensive line coach Clete Fischer would recall many years later. That wasn't surprising given Osborne's background. He had played quarterback in college and wide receiver in the NFL for two seasons. And under his direction as offensive coordinator, the Cornhuskers began to rely more heavily on the pass. The 1969 team gained more yards passing than rushing, for only the second time in school history, with the national championship teams in 1970 and 1971 balanced between the two. "We were throwing a lot then," said Guy Ingles, a senior split end who caught 33 passes for 603 yards and 8 touchdowns in 1970. "We were going to throw twenty to twenty-five times a game. We wanted to throw for 200 yards and rush for 250."

From 1971 through 1976, Nebraska led the Big Eight in passing four times and was ranked number eight nationally in 1972, on the strong left arm of quarterback Dave Humm. The sophomore from Las Vegas, Nevada, passed for a school-record 2,074 yards in his first varsity season, and by the time he left, as a fifth-round NFL draft pick of the Oakland Raiders, he held or shared a dozen school passing records. His favorite target was wingback Johnny Rodgers, who set school records with 55 receptions for 942 yards.

That was Rodgers' final season. Osborne became head coach the following year. Humm was still the quarterback, and he would be for Osborne's second season as well. "We ran basically the same plays and did the same things" they had done during Devaney's national championship seasons, said Osborne. "We threw the ball a whole lot. But some people thought we were drab and unexciting, and somehow, the coaching change had caused it." Part of the problem was efficiency. Counting bowl games, Humm threw for twenty-four touchdowns with twenty-six interceptions during his final two seasons.

Even so, Osborne remained committed to the pass. "I used to kid Tom, when he first became the head coach, all he wanted to do was throw the ball," said Jim Ross, the head freshman coach and an assistant athletic director at the time. The veteran assistants, among them Fischer and Mike Corgan, tried to convince Osborne to run "once in a while. But Tom wanted to throw it all the time," Ross said.

Osborne's propensity toward passing influenced the players he recruited, particularly the quarterbacks, one of whom was Vince Ferragamo, a prep All-American and prolific drop-back passer who played for brother Chris at Banning High School in Carson, California. Southern California was Osborne's recruiting area as a Devaney assistant and he tried to persuade Ferragamo to go to Nebraska out of high school. The movie-star handsome Ferragamo, however, picked California, where he spent two seasons, before the emergence of Steve Bartkowski caused him to relocate from Berkeley to Lincoln.

Under NCAA transfer rules, Ferragamo had to sit out the 1974 season, and he began the 1975 season as a backup to senior Terry Luck, who had seen little action because of three knee surgeries after starting for the freshman team. When Luck was sidelined by injury in the first quarter of the Oklahoma State game, Ferragamo came on to direct a 28–20 victory. He accounted for all of the touchdowns, passing for two and running for two and earned national player-of-the-week honors. He held the starting job for the

Nebraska led the Big Eight in passing with Vince Ferragamo at quarterback in 1976. (Courtesy UNL Photography)

remainder of the season, finishing with twelve touchdown passes and only five interceptions. The fifth was on his first pass in the Fiesta Bowl game against Arizona State, however, and an unhappy Osborne pulled him.

Ferragamo had a monster season as a senior in 1976, completing 145 of 254 passes for 2,071 yards and 20 touchdowns, with only 9 interceptions. He threw for four touchdowns in a game twice and directed a third-quarter comeback for a 27–24 victory against Texas Tech in the Astro-Bluebonnet Bowl. But fans weren't happy with a 9–3–1 record, particularly since one of the losses was to Oklahoma.

The Sooners were a source of frustration for Osborne. They threw only 2 passes in the 1976 game, the first with 3:30 remaining, when quarterback Thomas Lott handed the ball to Woodie Shepard, who threw it to split end Steve Rhodes for a 47-yard gain to the Nebraska 35 yard line. Then, on third-and-19 from the 34, quarterback Dean Blevins passed to Rhodes, who lateraled to Elvis Peacock for a 32-yard gain to the Cornhusker 2 yard line, setting up Peacock's winning touchdown with 38 seconds left.

The victory was Oklahoma's fifth in a row against Nebraska, including four under Osborne. The Sooners would extend their streak to six before a 17–14 Nebraska upset in 1978. Then they would win three more. Oklahoma always seemed to have "a quarterback with great option ability who would make a play to win. We had a hard time beating anybody with speed at quarterback," said Osborne, who had decided by 1976 that he needed to begin recruiting quarterbacks who could run. "We felt our quarterbacks had to be mobile." He was no longer interested in those who ran the 40-yard dash in 4.9 or slower.

Seeing Double

Nebraska Coach Bill Jennings had a surprise for Texas when the Longhorns visited Lincoln to open the 1959 season. Late in the fourth quarter, Nebraska lined up with two quarterbacks under center, Tom Kramer and Pat Fischer, who was actually the left halfback. The tandem quarterback alignment was intended to deceive the Longhorn defense, which wouldn't know which of the players was taking the snap. One went left and the other went right.

The Cornhuskers put together a drive that carried from their own 29 yard line to the Texas 40, with Fischer gaining 12 yards on 1 play, while Coach Darrell Royal yelled "illegal formation" from the Texas sideline. Though Nebraska wasn't penalized, referee Cliff Ogden went to the Cornhusker locker room following the game, and after consulting a rulebook, he notified Jennings that it was illegal.

The discussion between Jennings and Ogden became heated, with Jennings complaining that a clipping penalty nullifying what would have been a 92-yard punt return for a touchdown by Fischer shouldn't have been called. Still unconvinced, Jennings indicated he might use the tandem quarterback formation again. But he never did. Nebraska lost the Texas game 20–0.

Osborne recruited an option quarterback for the first time in 1976, Jeff Quinn from Ord, Nebraska. Quinn, who ran the 40 in 4.7, wouldn't see significant action until 1979. In the mean time Tom Sorley, who directed the upset of Oklahoma as a senior in 1978, was a drop-back passer and a "fair runner," said Osborne. "He could get you 8 yards, but he probably wasn't fast enough to go the distance."

Quinn was fast enough and so was Nate Mason, a member of the 1979 recruiting class. The 6'2", 175-pound Mason came from Greenville, Texas, along with high school teammate Ricky Simmons, a wide receiver. Mason hadn't drawn a lot of attention in leading his team to a 9–1 record and codistrict championship. But he had 4.5 speed in the 40-yard dash and he was athletic; his nickname was "Skate." By all indications he would be a good fit in the metamorphosis of Osborne's offense. Mason also was black, at a time when race was an issue regarding quarterbacks, not just at Nebraska but also in the college ranks in general and in the NFL, as well. Rarely were blacks given a chance to play quarterback, except in option offenses that depended little on the pass.

Mason wasn't Nebraska's first African-American quarterback. Two others had preceded him. Henry Woods came from Midland, Texas, and played just one varsity season at Nebraska, as a sophomore in 1963. He completed his only pass, good for 43 yards and a touchdown against Colorado. The Cornhuskers wouldn't recruit another black quarterback until 1973, Osborne's first season as head coach. Earl Everett came from Southeast High School in Kansas City, Missouri, where he had played for coach Bill Myles until his senior season, when Nebraska hired Myles as an assistant.

Everett saw action with the varsity as a true freshman, though hardly enough to earn a letter, and after backing up Humm as a sophomore, he was moved to wide receiver. The position switch had nothing to do with race, however, according to Myles, who also was black. Everett lacked consistency at quarterback, and, as Myles pointed out, he had fumbled a snap near the goal line late in a 21–20 loss at Wisconsin in the second game of the season—Humm had been sidelined by a hip pointer. In addition the Cornhuskers had a logjam at quarterback for 1975. Ferragamo became eligible, joining Luck, junior Ed Burns, and sophomores Sorley and Randy Garcia, who had sat out the 1974 season following knee surgery.

Mason appeared to be headed for a successful career as a quarterback. He was "potentially one of the best running quarterbacks ever to play at Nebraska," according to the 1980 Cornhusker media guide. He had rushed for 144 yards and 5 touchdowns in addition to completing 15 of 30 passes for 346 yards and 2 touchdowns, without an interception, in 5 freshman games. He would be the first African-American quarterback to start at Nebraska, but he would start only twice during his career. While he was learning the system as a backup in 1980, attention had turned to a much-heralded freshman from Fort Worth, Texas, who had been won in a recruiting battle with Oklahoma. His name was Turner Gill.

Tommie Frazier, who helped lead Nebraska to national championships in 1994 and 1995, was probably the definitive quarterback in Osborne's option-oriented offense, and Heisman Trophy winner Eric Crouch took the offense, which by then depended on the pass only for its surprise value, to another level under Osborne's hand-picked

Turner Gill is the standard by which Nebraska quarterbacks are measured. (Courtesy Huskers Illustrated*)*

successor, Frank Solich. But Gill set the standard by which Nebraska quarterbacks are measured. He was a seminal figure, and had Coach Barry Switzer persuaded him to go to Oklahoma, the course of Cornhusker history would have altered dramatically.

According to Steve Taylor when he arrived at Nebraska from San Diego, California, as the "next Turner Gill" in 1985, Gill broke the stereotype that black quarterbacks were only runners. Gill could have been a drop-back passer. During his career, he completed 54 percent of his passes for 3,317 yards and 34 touchdowns, with only 11 interceptions, throwing 125 consecutive passes without an interception during one stretch. He also rushed for 1,317 yards, a school record for a quarterback, averaging 4.5 yards per carry. He earned first-team all-conference three times and finished fourth in voting for the Heisman Trophy in 1983. And the bottom line was, he won. Nebraska's record when he started was 28–2, including 20–0 in conference play.

Gill might easily have ended up at Oklahoma. Growing up in Fort Worth, he was familiar with the Sooners. But "I didn't know about Nebraska," he said years later. "I really didn't." In addition the subject of race was brought up. He heard how Everett had been moved from quarterback to wide receiver. "My parents, my friends, and my coaches in high school all told me I'd regret going to Nebraska," Gill told the *Lincoln Journal and Star* six years after he completed his eligibility. "If I had listened to them, I prob-ably would have stayed near home in Texas or played at Oklahoma or somewhere. The perception was that since I was black, there was no way Nebraska was suddenly going to start a black quarterback for more than a game or two. My friends and family told me I'd become a defensive back."

Gill earned second-team all-city recognition as a defensive back his junior season at Arlington Heights High. He also played flanker as well as quarterback, the position at which he excelled his senior season. He was the city's offensive player of the year and codefensive player of the year as well as all-county. But he didn't earn all-state honors and he wasn't chosen for the Texas high school all-star game.

Nevertheless, he was a high-priority recruit for Nebraska and Oklahoma, even though the Sooners had a commitment from Ricky Byers from LaPorte, Texas. Some recruiting analysts considered Byers the number one option quarterback in the state. Texas also wanted Gill. But he dropped the Longhorns from his short list when they told him he would have to choose between football and baseball. After Gill signed a letter of intent with Nebraska, former Texas coach Darrell Royal said, "If I was still coaching and he got away, I'd be sick. He is really something."

Baseball was a significant issue. Gill was a shortstop and pitcher, although an elbow problem limited his pitching during his senior season in high school, and following graduation the Chicago White Sox drafted him as an infielder in the second round. He wanted $100,000 to sign, however, and the White Sox offered only $75,000. So Nebraska's recruiting efforts paid off.

The Cornhuskers assured him he could play baseball and so did Oklahoma. Recruits could sign two letters of intent in 1980, a conference letter and a national letter a week later. The day before conference letters could be signed, Gill called Switzer to say he had settled on Nebraska and there was no reason for the Sooner coach to make a planned final visit to his home in Fort Worth. Switzer didn't give up that easily, however. He visited Gill, as did his recruiting coordinator Scott Hill and baseball coach Enos Semore. But Gill held fast, spending more time that day with Cornhusker assistant Lance Van Zandt, a Texan.

Gill spent that night at the home of his high school coach, Merlin Priddy—at the urging of his parents. The next morning, he and Priddy ate breakfast at a local pancake house and then went to the high school, arriving at 7:57 A.M., just three minutes before letters could be officially signed. "I wasn't taking any chances," Priddy told the *Lincoln Journal and Star*. "Nebraska and Turner Gill is a perfect marriage." Oklahoma had "pulled hard on him," Priddy said. "Switzer told Turner he'd change his offense, if Turner would change his mind." Gill wasn't a Wishbone quarterback, said Priddy. "He's used to running and throwing." Nebraska's offense was "tailor-made" for him.

For Gill, Osborne was the determining factor. There was an immediate connection. "You didn't feel like he was arrogant, like, 'I'm the head coach at Nebraska.' He didn't come across that way," Gill said after he had returned to Nebraska as quarterbacks coach. "He was soft-spoken, sincere, and trustworthy."

By the end of his freshman season, spent on the freshman team, Gill had the full support of Cornhusker fans. Osborne gave him the option of redshirting his second season. With senior Mark Mauer and Mason ahead of him on the depth chart, he probably wouldn't get an opportunity to play unless one of those two were injured. Fans, however, were clamoring for Gill after Nebraska lost two of its first three games. There were letters to the editor calling for Osborne to give him a chance.

Gill's chance came, in part, at Mason's expense. After starting the second and third games in 1981, Mason was

George Flippin

I n 1892, two years after its first football team was organized, Nebraska was scheduled to play its first game as a member of the Western Inter-State University Football Association. The opponent was to be Missouri, and the game was to be played at Omaha. The problem was that Missouri refused to play because of Nebraska's George Flippin, who was African American. So the game was forfeited, 1–0.

Flippin was among the earliest black athletes at a predominantly white university, according to Arthur Ashe's exhaustive *A Hard Road to Glory.* Flippin, the son of a freed slave, earned three football letters at Nebraska and was elected team captain in 1894. He also was a heavyweight wrestling champion and competed for the track and field team, throwing the sixteen-pound hammer and putting the shot.

Flippin, who was born in Port Isabelle, Ohio, left the university and went to Chicago, where he earned a medical degree. He eventually returned to Nebraska, settling in Stromsburg and establishing a hospital with his father, Dr. C. A. Flippin, who had a medical practice in Grand Island.

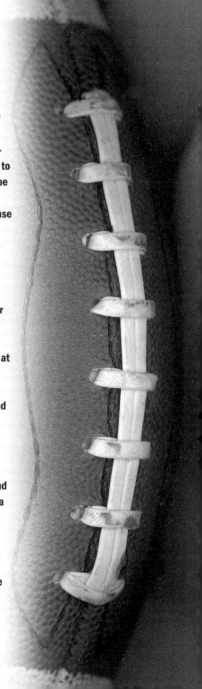

sidelined by an ankle problem that required surgery. Then, when Mauer was ineffective during the first half of the fourth game against Auburn, Osborne turned to Gill. The Cornhuskers left a rain-soaked field at halftime trailing 3–0, to a smattering of boos from the crowd at Memorial Stadium. But they rallied behind Gill, winning 17–3. The next week, he responded to the challenge of his first start by throwing four touchdown passes, tying a school record, in a 59–0 victory over Colorado.

Had Gill gone to Oklahoma, Nebraska football history would have been changed, just as it would have been changed had he signed with the White Sox out of high school. And there would be two more potential turning points, the first near the end of his sophomore season, the second before his senior season.

In the first quarter of the next-to-last game of the 1981 regular season against Iowa State, Gill suffered a calf injury. The next day, he underwent what was reported as "minor surgery" to drain blood from the badly swollen calf. Though he would miss the final regular-season game against Oklahoma, there was hope he would be able to play in a bowl game. But the injury didn't heal as expected and a month later a specialist prescribed a second surgery, which revealed a more serious nerve problem, one that could jeopardize Gill's career. If the nerve didn't regenerate properly, he wouldn't be able to play. "Everybody got into the act," head trainer and physical therapist George Sullivan told the *Lincoln Journal and Star*. "Every quack in the nation wanted to treat him. People were telling the doctors to use everything from grape peels and Southern stump water to healing herbs in the back room."

Nebraska's backfield in 1981 and 1982 included both Roger Craig (left) and Mike Rozier (right). Former Cornhusker Charlie Greene, an Olympic sprinter, is seated in the middle. (Courtesy Huskers Illustrated)

Gill came back not through such home remedies but rather through dedicated rehabilitation, helped along by former Cornhusker defensive tackle Bill Barnett, who had suffered a similar injury playing for the NFL's Miami Dolphins that season. The two encouraged each other, and though he was held out of contact during spring practice, Gill was ready to go by the 1982 opener. But for a 27–24 loss at Penn State, the Cornhuskers would have won a national championship his junior season.

With that as a backdrop, Nebraska and Penn State were to be matched in the first Kickoff Classic to open the 1983 season. But Osborne was hesitant to accept the invitation after Gill announced at the Big Eight baseball tournament in Oklahoma City that he might be willing to sign a baseball contract and forgo his senior season. He hadn't played baseball as a freshman because of a mix-up in credit hours, and he had missed his sophomore season because of the leg injury. But his play at shortstop as a junior showed that he still possessed the skills in which the White Sox had once been interested.

Initially, he told Osborne that he was 90 percent certain that he would play his senior season at Nebraska. In Oklahoma City, however, he described it as a 50–50 proposition. Seeing all of the big-league scouts at the tournament had gotten him "all hyped up about baseball," he told *Huskers Illustrated.* "People in Nebraska can't realize . . . that there's another sport in my life." By the time the draft came, however, he had announced he was staying at Nebraska, much to the relief of Osborne, as well as Cornhusker fans. The New York Yankees selected him as an afterthought in the eighteenth round.

Nebraska was ranked number one from the beginning to the end of the regular season, with the "Scoring Explosion" offense featuring the "triplets": I-back Mike Rozier, wingback Irving Fryar, and Gill. Rozier would win the Heisman Trophy and be the first selection in the NFL's supplemental draft, while Fryar would be the first selection in the regular draft. More than anyone, however, Gill ignited the explosion, which came within a tipped, two-point conversion pass of winning a national championship.

Looking back years later, Gill said he didn't remember exactly whether Oklahoma had been among the schools that told him he wouldn't get to play quarterback at Nebraska because of his race. "But it was an issue," he said. "I had the approach that one day Nebraska would have a black quarterback, so why not me? I wasn't saying it would be me, just that it could be." And it was, changing the direction of the program as no other player before or since.

Outlandish Linemen

Nebraska had defeated Oklahoma 73–21 in early November 1996 and the Cornhuskers were flying back to Lincoln when Coach Tom Osborne placed a recruiting call to Dominic Raiola. "I thought somebody was playing a joke on me. 'Really, is this Coach Osborne?'" Raiola recalled later. Osborne confirmed that he was, indeed, Nebraska's coach. "I was pretty impressed with that," said Raiola, who would leave his home in Honolulu, Hawaii, to play for the Cornhuskers. He was Nebraska's first scholarship recruit from the Aloha State.

Some might question the wisdom of such a move. Raiola couldn't surf in Nebraska. But he had decided early on that he wasn't going to play for Hawaii. "I knew I was going to go away. It didn't matter how far," he said. "I wanted to go to the best program. And I knew winning was a big thing here at Nebraska." The Cornhuskers had just won back-to-back national championships, and they would win a third when Raiola was a redshirt freshman in what would be Osborne's final season as coach. Plus, Nebraska's tradition of producing outstanding offensive linemen was appealing. He played guard and tackle at perennial power St. Louis High, which didn't lose in his final three seasons, extending a string of state titles to eleven.

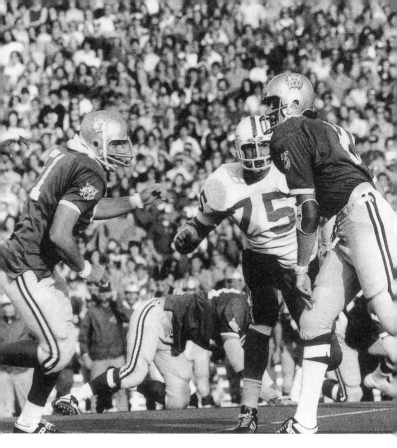

Defensive tackle Larry Jacobson (75) was Nebraska's first Outland Trophy winner in 1971. (Courtesy UNL Photography)

During his three seasons at Nebraska, before leaving early for the NFL, Raiola established a place among those linemen, earning All-America recognition as a center in 2000. He also was a finalist for both the Lombardi Award and the Outland Trophy. He was "particularly" disappointed at not winning the Outland, Cornhusker offensive line coach Milt Tenopir said. "I think we all were."

The Burr Oak

Dean Steinkuhler said he would have walked on at Nebraska if he hadn't been offered a scholarship. Though other schools had shown some recruiting interest, among them Kansas State and Arizona State, he had grown up in the tiny southeast Nebraska community of Burr, listening to the legendary Lyell Bremser's radio broadcasts of Nebraska football games. He might have dreamed of playing for the Cornhuskers someday. But with a population of 110, Burr wasn't on the itinerary of most recruiters.

Steinkuhler attended kindergarten through eighth grade in a four-room country school, then went to high school in nearby Sterling, where he played eight-man football as a senior. His senior season, he was a fullback on offense, used primarily as a blocker and didn't earn a place on the all-conference first team. But he attracted enough attention that the *Lincoln Sunday Journal and Star* named him its eight-man player of the year. Even so, "I wasn't a great player in high school," he told the *Omaha World-Herald*. "I don't know if Nebraska ever thought I'd make it. But they gave me a chance."

The 6'3" Steinkuhler played offensive guard at Nebraska. He weighed 225 pounds when he arrived and bulked up to 270 by the time he was a fifth-year senior, without losing his speed. He ran the fastest 40-yard dash in Cornhusker history by an offensive lineman, an electronically timed 4.87 seconds.

As a senior he earned Nebraska's third consecutive Outland Trophy and its second consecutive Lombardi Award. Ken Denlinger, a columnist for the *Washington Post,* wrote that Steinkuhler rather than teammate Mike Rozier deserved the Heisman Trophy as college football's best player. He also earned the distinction of being the consensus football All-American from the smallest hometown since World War II, edging out Bruce Bosley, an All-American at West Virginia in 1955. Bosley's hometown, Green Bank, West Virginia, had a population of 115.

The Football Writers Association of America presents the Outland Trophy to the nation's outstanding interior lineman. The trophy dates to 1946. And Nebraska's trophy case has eight, twice as many as any other school. The Cornhuskers' first two went to defensive linemen, tackle Larry Jacobson in 1971 and middle guard Rich Glover a year later. But their last six have gone to offensive linemen, including two to Dave Rimington, like Raiola a center, and the trophy's only two-time winner.

Rimington set the standard for offensive linemen, not just at Nebraska but at the collegiate level as well. In addition to the back-to-back Outland Trophies, he also won the Lombardi Award as a senior in 1982, and he finished fifth in voting for the Heisman Trophy. He was a two-time consensus All-American, a two-time Academic All-American, and, oh yes, as a junior he was an overwhelming choice as the Big Eight Offensive Player of the Year, even though he never carried, caught, or passed the ball. After the Cincinnati Bengals made Rimington a first-round draft pick in 1983, offensive line coach Jim McNally said if one were to design the perfect center, he wouldn't be better than Rimington, who could get under nose tackles, being fast enough to get to them and strong enough to block them.

Rimington was the first of Nebraska's Outland Trophy–winning offensive linemen, with the first of his two coming as a surprise. His goal in 1981, his second season as a starter, was to be the first-team all-conference center, an honor he expected to go to Missouri's Brad Edelman. Winning a second Outland was less surprising, assuming he didn't lose his focus, because of the recognition he had already earned.

Nebraska's tradition of outstanding offensive linemen has included Dominic Raiola (54) and Toniu Fonoti (77), both All-Americans from Hawaii. (Courtesy Huskers Illustrated*)*

Teammate Dean Steinkuhler succeeded Rimington as the Outland Trophy winner in 1983. He also won the Lombardi Award. The Cornhuskers wouldn't have another Outland Trophy winner until 1992, when Will Shields won it. Zach Wiegert and Aaron Taylor succeeded Shields in quick succession, in 1994 and 1997. Teammate Jason Peter,

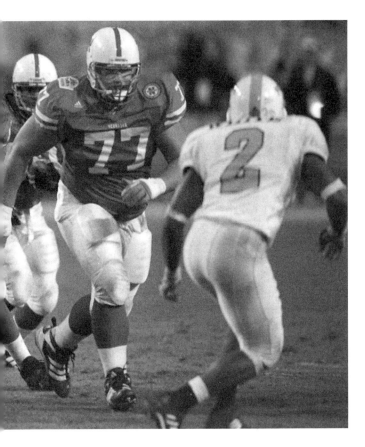

a defensive tackle, was a finalist for the award when Taylor won it.

Taylor played offensive guard in 1997, after earning All-America honors as a center in 1996, extending a tradition that dates to 1932, when Lawrence Ely became the first of Nebraska's twelve All-America centers, including two besides Rimington who achieved that status twice. Rik Bonness was an All-America center in 1974 and 1975, and Jake Young was an All-American in 1988 and 1989.

Because of that tradition, "everyone wanted to play center at Nebraska," Bill Lewis said of his decision to accept Osborne's scholarship offer out of high school in Sioux City, Iowa, in 1981. He earned All-America recognition at the position in 1985, fast on the heels of Mark Traynowicz in 1984. Lewis credited the Cornhuskers' system for developing not just centers but offensive linemen in general. With the benefit of numbers, created by walk-on players, "nobody ever stood around" during practice, said Lewis. "You got to rep the hell out of plays. That was absolutely essential to Nebraska's success. I don't know if another program in the country had that. There was nothing close in the NFL."

Lewis played in seven NFL seasons, after earning a job as a seventh-round draft pick of the Oakland Raiders in 1986. Only four other players selected after the fifth round, including free agents, survived the final cut that year, according to Lewis. Nebraska had prepared him well.

The same could be said of Raiola and Toniu Fonoti, another Hawaii recruit who earned All-America recognition at offensive guard and was an Outland Trophy finalist in 2001. Fonoti, like Raiola, left Nebraska for the NFL following his junior season. Five days after the Cornhuskers lost 37–14 to Miami in the Rose Bowl game, Fonoti called Tenopir to say he would be leaving. Fonoti placed the call at 6:30 in the morning Hawaii time, an indication that he had difficulty sleeping. Tenopir was "a little surprised" and bothered by the fact that the decision had been based on the potential for injury during his senior season. "I think he had a little feedback from folks that he's healthy now [so] he'd better do it," Tenopir said. "That's a wrong mindset. We've had how many linemen that have gone through here that have played NFL ball that have finished it out?"

The answer at that point was all had finished out except Raiola, who left the previous year, after being the recipient of the first Rimington Trophy as the nation's top collegiate center. The trophy is sponsored by the Boomer Esiason Foundation, of which Rimington is the president. Two decades before Raiola and Fonoti bypassed their senior seasons, however, another award-winning Cornhusker offensive lineman considered leaving for the NFL after his junior year, and for reasons similar to Fonoti's. The player in question was Rimington.

Buses were waiting the night of January 2, 1982, outside Miami's Brickell Point Holiday Inn to take the Nebraska football team to a post–Orange Bowl game dinner at a local country club. The night before, the Cornhuskers had suffered a frustrating loss to top-ranked Clemson. As it turned out, a national championship had been at stake. Although Nebraska was ranked number four going into the game, those ahead of it had lost that day, third-ranked Alabama to Texas in the Cotton Bowl and second-ranked Georgia to Pittsburgh in the Sugar Bowl.

The Cornhuskers were hardly in a socializing mood. Everyone was a little on edge, if not irritable. Sophomore I-back Mike Rozier had been excused from attending the Orange Bowl–sponsored function so he could fly home to Camden, New Jersey. The Big Eight offensive newcomer of the year would consider staying there because he was so discouraged about how his first season at Nebraska had ended. His attitude was characteristic, though perhaps more extreme.

While the engines of the buses idled, Osborne and Rimington talked in the hotel lobby, a less-than-amicable exchange that delayed the team's departure. The subject

Centers of Attention

Coach W. C. "Bummy" Booth's Cornhuskers won twenty-five consecutive games from 1901 to 1903. His 1902 team posted a 9–0 record and didn't allow a point. Included in those nine victories was Nebraska's first against mighty Minnesota, by 6–0 at Minneapolis in mid-October, before an audience reported to be 6,000. Johnny Bender scored the winning touchdown—worth five points at the time—with barely five of the game's seventy minutes remaining. Maurice Benedict converted the extra point.

The Cornhuskers center that day was a young Omahan named Charles Borg, the "first of the line of great centers," *Omaha World-Herald* sports editor Frederick Ware would write nearly forty years later. That line now includes twelve who have earned All-America honors.

Lawrence Ely (Grand Island, Neb.) 1932
Charles Brock (Columbus, Neb.) 1938
Tom Novak (Omaha, Neb.) 1949
Rik Bonness (Bellevue, Neb.) 1974–75
Tom Davis (Omaha, Neb.) 1977
Dave Rimington (Omaha, Neb.) 1981–82
Mark Traynowicz (Bellevue, Neb.) 1984
Bill Lewis (Sioux City, Iowa) 1985
Jake Young (Midland, Tex.) 1988–89
Aaron Graham (Denton, Tex.) 1995
Aaron Taylor (Wichita Falls, Tex.) 1996*
Dominic Raiola (Honolulu, Hawaii) 2000
*Earned All-America honors as a guard in 1997.

was Rimington's interest in investigating the possibility of bypassing his senior season and submitting his name for the NFL draft. Rimington hadn't achieved all of his goals. He wanted to contribute to Nebraska's first national championship since Bob Devaney's teams earned back-to-back titles about the time he became interested in the Cornhuskers. But he had piled up plenty of individual awards and established himself as the best center in the country. During the telecast of the Orange Bowl game, NBC's Don Criqui said NFL scouts considered him the best player in college football, regardless of position.

During his travels to receive his many awards before the Orange Bowl game, Rimington had been encouraged by several people to consider turning pro, among them Sean Farrell, an All-America offensive guard at Penn State who would be a first-round pick of the Tampa Bay Buccaneers in the 1982 NFL draft. Several of Rimington's teammates also suggested he at least look into the possibility. He had the support of the offensive line, he said. He didn't have the support of Osborne or his position coaches, Tenopir and Clete Fischer, however. And that led to the impromptu meeting in the hotel lobby. "It sounds mercenary, but it happens. I really have mixed feelings," Rimington told the *Lincoln Journal*. His concerns were practical. He had played much of his junior season with an ailing knee, and "right now, my knee is stable enough to play without corrective surgery," he said. There was no guarantee it would remain that way if he were to play another season at Nebraska.

He wouldn't have been in a position to consider leaving early if not for a knee injury suffered in the Nebraska Shrine Bowl all-star game following his senior year in high school. He began his first season at Nebraska on the freshman team but quickly moved up to the varsity and played late in the first home game against Hawaii, a rare opportunity for a true freshman. But he aggravated the knee injury and was sidelined for the remainder of the season, following surgery. As a result, the Big Eight granted him a medical hardship, which meant even though he was a junior in eligibility, he was in his fourth year.

The rules about drafting college underclassmen were more stringent then than they are now. Herschel Walker had considered challenging the NFL rule after his sophomore season in 1981. But he remained at Georgia and won the Heisman Trophy in 1982 before leaving to play in the short-lived United States Football League. If Rimington, an Academic All-American, could complete his degree in business administration before the NFL season began, however, he could declare for the draft.

When he and Osborne had words, Rimington thought he could earn enough credits during the spring semester and summer sessions to complete his degree before NFL training camps began. But he had miscalculated. Realistically, he couldn't finish in time. So three days after the Orange Bowl game, in a statement released by the Nebraska sports information office, he announced that he was staying and that he would undergo surgery to repair the knee problem.

Some had questioned his loyalty for even thinking about leaving early. But such doubt wasn't deserved. He became interested in the Cornhuskers when he was nine years old and grew up with Devaney's successful teams and the seamless coaching transition to Osborne. When he was a 6'2", 200-pound ninth-grader, he caught the attention of

Big Jake

L arry Jacobson, the Cornhuskers' first Outland Trophy winner as a senior on the 1971 national championship team, didn't even earn All-Big Eight honorable mention as a junior. So the 6'7", 247-pound defensive tackle from Sioux Falls, South Dakota, was surprised when he got a phone call from Monte Kiffin, his position coach, to tell him he had won the Outland Trophy. Kiffin also "had to tell me how to spell it," recalled Jacobson, an All-American and finalist for the Lombardi Award, too, in 1971.

John Faiman, the varsity football coach at Omaha South High School. Faiman, a quarterback at Nebraska in the early 1960s, saw him jogging on the track one day and mistook him for a student at what is now the University of Nebraska-Omaha.

Rimington started at center and defensive tackle—he preferred defense—for Faiman at South as a sophomore but suffered a broken right leg in the first game as a junior and missed the rest of the season. When Rimington was a high school senior, he earned all-state and all-metro honors as a lineman. He was the Stockmen's 400 Club "Lineman of the Year" and the Omaha B'Nai B'rith "Athlete of the Year." But he wasn't necessarily the best-known athlete at South High. His classmates included gymnast Jim Hartung, who would go on to be a two-time Olympian.

Both he and Hartung accepted scholarships from Nebraska. Rimington might have gone elsewhere. Had he been from a metropolitan area in another state, Osborne said, he would have been heavily recruited by most of the top programs. Such was his potential. But loyalty precluded serious consideration of other schools. A factor in picking Nebraska was his wanting "to be recognized in my home state," he said. "It drives you to be a better player. Most of the time you've got to have pressure. You can't be in a comfort zone."

Rimington's recruiting class provided the basis for one of the best offensive lines in school history in 1982. His group didn't draw the attention of the 1994 "Pipeline," with Wiegert, the Outland Trophy winner, and Rob Zatechka at tackles, Brenden Stai and Joel Wilks at guards, and Aaron Graham at center, or even the 1995 "Pipeline II," which included Taylor, a future Outland Trophy winner, and all new starters except Graham. Both those lines cleared the way for national championships; the 1982 team came one controversial loss at Penn State from winning Osborne's first national title.

The 1982 team was arguably Osborne's best prior to the national championship run because it was better defensively than the "Scoring Explosion" team that followed, and its offensive statistics were impressive except when compared with those of its immediate successor. It was "probably the best team I've been on, maybe some of the pro teams, too," Rimington said fifteen years later. "They scored more points in 1983, but I think we had more maturity in the offensive line. We had five refrigerators."

Rimington was the biggest, at 6'3" and 290 pounds. But he depended on more than just size and strength. He was quick. "Most teams come off the ball together," an opposing noseguard told a Lincoln newspaper. "He comes off the

Dave Rimington is the only player to win the Outland Trophy twice. He also won the Lombardi Award, was a two-time All-American, and was the Big Eight Conference "Offensive Player of the Year" as a center in 1981. (Courtesy Huskers Illustrated)

ball, takes three steps, and 'bam!' Then the rest of the line moves." And he was smart, handling the line calls. His ability to make adjustments was illustrated in a 6–0 victory at Missouri during his junior season. The Cornhuskers broke the scoreless tie with only 23 seconds remaining, when fullback Phil Bates finished off a 10-play, 64-yard drive that had begun with 2:36 left. Throughout the game, the Missouri defense blitzed quarterback Turner Gill in an attempt to fluster the sophomore in only his third start. The alignment placed players on Rimington's shoulders. He would block the defender on the left and the pulling guard would "split" the defender on the right. Rimington changed the play in the huddle so that instead of splitting the defenders, he and the guard would both block down. He told Bates to look for an opening to the left. Bates did, and he got the final 3 yards.

During their weekly teleconference that season, Big Eight coaches were asked if they could have one player in the conference to build a team, who would it be? Three of the coaches picked Rimington.

He was the foundation of the 1982 line, which included Randy Theiss and Jeff Kwapick at the tackles and Steinkuhler and Mike Mandelko at the guards. All were fifth-year seniors, members of that 1978 recruiting class, except Steinkuhler, who was a fourth-year junior. In Nebraska's time-tested system, freshmen played on a freshman-junior varsity team then sat out a redshirt season before contributing. Prior to 1978 the NCAA didn't allow the redshirting of freshmen. With that change Nebraska's system began to change. Most programs dropped their freshman teams and Nebraska was forced to follow suit.

In 1982 Rimington and Theiss were in their third seasons as starters and Mandelko was in his second, as was Steinkuhler. They were a confident bunch, "blue-collar guys who worked their butts off every day in practice," according to Rimington, under the watchful eyes of Tenopir and Fischer, whose raspy voice sounded a little like that of the Penguin in the *Batman* television series, Burgess Meredith. Fischer, who worked mostly with the centers and guards, would identify players by number and sometimes by hometown, if they were from Nebraska. He was responsible for recruiting the state and knew hometowns. He rarely referred to them by name. So Rimington was "number 50" or "Omaha."

Offensive linemen are bigger nowadays. But Nebraska's line in 1982 was good-sized for its time. Mandelko was the shortest at 6'2" and the lightest at 255 pounds, about the same as Kwapick and Theiss. Rimington had little use for small quick linemen. "I don't see the purpose unless you're going to run a race," he said. "All you've got is about a 5-yard box." And they controlled that box.

Their self-assurance combined with their size could be intimidating. They never ran from the huddle to the line of scrimmage, said Rimington. "We just walked up, got in our stance, and took care of business," with socks pulled down and jerseys rolled up to expose massive forearms and biceps. Arms couldn't be covered, an unwritten rule among them, even on a blustery day with frigid temperatures like the one at Iowa State in 1982. The linemen covered their arms in Vaseline to prevent numbness, all except Kwapick, who opted for an undershirt with sleeves beneath his jersey. "He did things his own way," Rimington said. "He was the sane one." They also "double-taped" their jerseys to their pads for

Anticipate This

To compensate for his lack of speed, Kelly Saalfeld would anticipate the snap count. When the quarterback drew in his breath, "I started the snap," said Saalfeld, who walked on to become a first-team all-conference center for the Cornhuskers in 1979. Coach Tom Osborne's offensive system used a rhythmic count rather than a hard count, so his anticipating the snap worked, Saalfeld said.

When he tried it during a practice with the New York Giants, however, it didn't. The Giants used a hard count, which resulted in second-year quarterback Phil Simms fumbling the snap. Simms proceeded to pick up the ball and fire it at his posterior, said Saalfeld, who described it as a "Preparation H" pass.

a tighter fit, a technique that was more functional than aesthetic because it made grabbing them by the jersey difficult for defensive linemen. Rimington learned the double-taping technique from Pittsburgh's Jimbo Covert and Dan Marino, whom he had met at All-America functions. Marino wanted to know if he lived on a farm. "He thought all of us [from Nebraska] live on farms, that we're all big plowboys," Rimington said.

Covert and Marino also showed him another technique for frustrating those who tried to get an edge by grabbing offensive linemen in order to move them out of the way—spraying WD-40 or a similar lubricant over their pads. Before the game, the linemen, in full gear, would step in the shower area of the locker room and "spray that stuff on each other," said Rimington. "It was probably toxic in a closed area. But we wanted to do whatever it took." The rules prohibit the use of such lubrication now.

Ironically, Rimington was at the center of a holding controversy prior to his senior season. The *Denver Post* reported that Big Eight game officials were shown film clips of his techniques for grabbing defenders during a preseason clinic. Bruce Finlayson, the Big Eight supervisor of officials, denied that. "I don't think he holds that much," Finlayson told the *Lincoln Star*. "He's a good player and knocks people around. He's just an All-American, that's all. He beats his man. People like to use holding as an excuse." The report might have stemmed from complaints by Colorado coach Chuck Fairbanks, Finlayson added.

Tenopir told the *Star* that someone was "trying to put the ax to" Rimington because he "just might be the best football player in the conference. He's so dadgum overpowering, he's whipped most anybody he's come up against," said Tenopir. "You might think he's holding even though he isn't."

That might have explained why the Southeastern Conference officials who worked the Orange Bowl game against Clemson called Rimington for holding twice and clipping once during the first half. Clemson alternated middle guards William Devane and William Petty against Rimington in seventy-seven-degree heat and 74 percent humidity. They finished with one tackle between them. Afterward, Osborne said he wasn't pointing a finger at the officials, but Rimington had rarely been penalized during the season and to be flagged three times in the first half was surprising. Coach and player were frustrated with how things had gone. And it spilled over to their discussion the next day.

Heisman Trio

Johnny Rodgers became Nebraska's first Heisman Trophy winner in 1972, thirty-seven years after the Downtown Athletic Club of New York City established the award, finishing well ahead of runner-up Greg Pruitt of Oklahoma in the balloting. "I think they made a mistake," the United Press International quoted Pruitt after the results were announced, even though he and Rodgers were friends. Rodgers's numbers were compelling, but because of some off-the-field issues, the Cornhusker wingback wasn't considered a lock to win the award as college football's best player. But Rodgers easily out-distanced Pruitt and third-place finisher Rich Glover, a Nebraska teammate.

There was considerably less suspense when Mike Rozier took home the trophy in 1983. The Cornhusker I-back was only the second player in NCAA Division I-A history to rush for more than 2,000 yards in a season—the first, USC's Marcus Allen, had won the Heisman two years before. Actually, Rozier didn't take the trophy to his home. It went to his mom's home. He handled it only briefly at the presentation ceremony, handing it to his brother and Nebraska teammate Guy Rozier, who handed it to their mom, Beatrice. "I always said I'd give this to my mom if I won it," Mike said. "On behalf of the Downtown Athletic Club and me, Mom, this trophy is for you." Rozier added with a characteristic smile, "Don't drop it, Mom. It was hard to get."

Johnny Rodgers, Eric Crouch, and Mike Rozier (left to right) at the Heisman Trophy presentation ceremony in 2001. (Courtesy Huskers Illustrated*)*

Eric Crouch, Nebraska's third winner, had prepared himself for the disappointment of not hearing his name called in 2001, at the first Heisman Trophy presentation ceremony not held at the Downtown Athletic Club. In the aftermath of the September 11 terrorist attack on the World Trade Center, the club was closed and the ceremony was moved to the Marriott Marquis in Manhattan. Crouch, among four quarterbacks invited to the ceremony, edged Florida's Rex Grossman, with Miami's Ken Dorsey a relatively close third and Oregon's Joey Harrington fourth. A week later, Crouch was back in Lincoln, and the trophy was sitting on a counter in his apartment. There was no other place to put it, said Crouch, because the apartment was so small.

Johnny Rodgers

The numbers couldn't be ignored. Johnny Rodgers did everything during his senior season. He caught 55 passes for 942 yards and 8 touchdowns. He rushed 58 times for 308 yards and 2 touchdowns. He averaged 15.8 yards and scored 2 touchdowns on 39 punt returns. And he averaged 23 yards on 8 kickoff returns. Plus, he contributed to three Big Eight titles and back-to-back national championships as a sophomore and junior, when he earned consensus All-America honors. "Johnny Rodgers probably could impact a football game in more ways than anyone I've been involved with," Tom Osborne once said. If not for Rodgers's kick returns, and the threat they posed, Nebraska might not have won the two national titles, according to Osborne.

Rodgers's signature season was probably the second, on a team that still ranks among the best all-time in college football. And his signature play came in what was billed as the "Game of the Century," a 35–31 victory at Oklahoma before a national television audience on Thanksgiving Day 1971. Less than five minutes into the first quarter, Rodgers fielded a Joe Wylie punt; avoided a tackle attempt by Greg Pruitt, the first Sooner with a shot at him; and raced 72 yards for a touchdown, setting the tone for the afternoon's drama. A year later, *Sports Illustrated*'s Dan Jenkins would describe the 5'9", 173-pound wingback as possibly "the most devastating player ever suited up" for his size.

Jenkins's words focused national attention on Rodgers that even his numbers, however compelling, could not, helping to shape national opinion the way ESPN's *Sports-Center* highlights do now. So Jenkins assisted Rodgers in becoming Nebraska's first Heisman Trophy winner. Heisman ballots would be "going into the mails soon," Jenkins wrote, to 1,200 voters, and the choice was clear. If Rodgers "is not this season's leading candidate (if not, in fact, the only candidate) then most of the writers must be planning on writing in the names of their cousins."

The *Sports Illustrated* story was published less than a month before the trophy presentation and might have nudged those who were hesitant to vote for Rodgers because of off-the-field problems, most notably his involvement in an armed robbery in the spring of his freshman year. He received two years' probation for the $91 robbery, which he described as a "prank," and his driver's license was suspended. Before his senior season, he ran a stop sign while driving with the suspended license, drawing more negative publicity and, eventually, a sentence of thirty days in jail. However, "Rodgers' past is not all that evil, despite the fact that Nebraska's opponents would have the world believe that he is a mini-Capone during the off-season," wrote Jenkins, who noted that Rodgers had attempted to make amends.

A majority of Heisman voters agreed with Jenkins. Rodgers's name was first on 301 ballots, compared with runner-up Pruitt's 117. The player that Cornhusker radio broadcast legend Lyell Bremser first called "Johnny the Jet" received 1,310 voting points to Pruitt's 966. Nebraska teammate and friend Rich Glover, a middle guard, finished third, with 99 first-place votes and 652 total points. Rodgers stayed with Glover in Jersey City, New Jersey, when he attended the Heisman Trophy presentation ceremony. Glover, also a senior, won the Outland Trophy and Lombardi Award in 1972.

State senator Ernie Chambers, who has been the state's racial conscience for more than three decades, introduced a resolution in the Nebraska Legislature praising Rodgers, who had "climbed the highest mountain and reached the pinnacle," the *Lincoln Journal* quoted Chambers. Rodgers had been "pilloried in the press and made the butt of many unkind jokes," Chambers said. Race was a factor. Rodgers grew up in north Omaha, in difficult circumstances. Those who didn't know his background, thought "everything was hunky-dory," he said, adding, jokingly, that his size was a result of "sipping soup through a straw" from fighting every weekend. "My jaws were sore."

His athletic success at Omaha Technical High School—which also graduated, among others, baseball Hall of Famer Bob Gibson—made him a target of neighborhood toughs. "Nobody ever shot anybody. The mentality has changed," Rodgers said. However, they "would hurt you, beat you up. People were jumping on me. When it was one-on-one, I proved to be tougher than they thought." But when it was more than one, as was often the case, "I had to get up and run." That's how he developed his unique ability as a kick returner, he said, on the streets of north Omaha. Escaping those who were intent on doing him serious physical harm was tougher than eluding tacklers in the open field.

He earned prep All-America honors in football at Tech and was a talented enough baseball player that the Los

Angeles Dodgers drafted him. But he envisioned a future in football, specifically as a running back at Southern California, where the 1968 Heisman Trophy winner, O. J. Simpson, had played. If Trojans Coach John McKay had offered him a scholarship, "there wouldn't have been much Coach [Bob] Devaney could have said. There probably wouldn't have been anything anybody could have done" to get him to go to Nebraska, he said. "I wanted to go there."

Rodgers, who was selected by fans as the Cornhusker of the century, never lost interest in playing running back. With him at I-back instead of wingback, Nebraska might have won an unprecedented third consecutive national championship in 1972, he has said, pointing to his performance in a 40–6 victory against Notre Dame in the 1973 Orange Bowl game, his last as a Cornhusker. In a surprise move devised by Osborne and sanctioned by Devaney, he started at I-back and responded by rushing for three touchdowns, throwing a halfback pass for a touchdown and catching a touchdown pass. The performance was definitely Heisman Trophy quality. "I think he got more publicity and that helped," Pruitt told the UPI's Milton Richman in explaining why he rather than Rodgers should have won the award as the nation's best collegiate player. If so, Jenkins probably deserved some of the credit for that.

Mike Rozier

The Memorial Stadium crowd of 76,387 stood and applauded Mike Rozier as trainers George Sullivan and Jerry Weber helped him from the field with 2:50 remaining in the third quarter of a 48–10 victory against Oklahoma State in early November 1982. The junior I-back's legs were

Mike Rozier runs to daylight against Oklahoma, with help from two-time Outland Trophy winner Dave Rimington (50). (Courtesy Huskers Illustrated*)*

cramping. He had a sore wrist. And to top it off, he had to deal with the throbbing pain of a hip pointer.

On the play that sent him to the sideline, he had been tackled for a 3-yard loss. And with Nebraska leading 35–7, there was no reason to think he would return that afternoon. When he got to the sideline, however, teammates Roger Craig and Irving Fryar told him he was only 20 yards short of breaking the Cornhusker single-season rushing record. The record, held by Bobby Reynolds, was thirty-two years old. He should go back in, Craig and Fryar said.

Early in the fourth quarter, with barely time to catch his breath, Rozier returned to action, knowing that given the score, he wouldn't get many more carries. He gained 4 yards, then 13. Someone in the huddle said he needed 3 more for the record. On the next play he gained 2. His final carry, and thirty-third of the game, came on a counter-sweep, with guard Mike Mandelko and tackle Randy Theiss pulling, left to right. One Cowboy defender had a clear shot at him but missed. Another got a hand on his shoulder pads but couldn't pull him down. Rozier gained the yard he needed, and 36 more for good measure, on the way to the end zone and his fourth touchdown of the afternoon.

He finished with 251 rushing yards, to bring his season's total to a record 1,379. Had it been up to him, he would have stayed in the game long enough to break the school single-game record of 255 yards rushing. But "one record a day is enough," said Mike Corgan, his position coach. Rozier would have to wait a year before shattering that record, on the way to shattering the single-season rushing record he had just set, getting 1,689 yards by the end of the 1982 season.

Such performances became commonplace during Rozier's three seasons at Nebraska. He rushed for 200 or more yards 7 times, with a high of 285 against Kansas in 1983. But the game that characterized the Cornhuskers' second Heisman Trophy winner might have been a 23–19 victory against Missouri in 1982, two weeks before the record-breaking effort against Oklahoma State.

Rozier wasn't expected to play because of the hip pointer, but early in the second quarter, with Craig sidelined by an ankle injury and sophomore Jeff Smith ineffective, he went in. He wore a flak jacket to protect the hip, but the jacket was too bulky and he took it off at halftime. Though each breath was painful, he gained 66 of the 79 yards on what proved to be the winning drive late in the fourth quarter.

After back-up quarterback Bruce Mathison ran 16 yards for the final touchdown, Rozier went to the sideline, asked for an ice bag for his hip, and limped off the field before time elapsed. He spent more than a half-hour in the training room before Sullivan, the head trainer and physical therapist, helped him to his locker, where reporters waited. Sullivan made sure the interview was short. Across the room, defensive end Tony Felici imitated the reporters, beginning a question with, "Tell me, Mr. Rozier . . . " Rozier tried to stifle a laugh. It hurt too much.

Even though he predicted he would break the single-game rushing record and did in his final home game in 1983, Rozier was never motivated by individual accomplishments. "A national championship would mean more to me than a Heisman Trophy," he said prior to that senior season. "I'd rather rush for 20 yards and win than rush for 200 yards and lose." By then, no one questioned his sincerity. What was originally regarded as disdain for the media was really just discomfort over being the center of attention.

He came from Camden, New Jersey, with humility and a sense of humor that belied his toughness and tolerance for pain. During his recruiting visit, he and the other prospective recruits were listening to a presentation by strength and conditioning coach Boyd Epley, who announced that "the best running back in the country is here with us today." Rozier looked around to check out his competition at I-back if he decided to sign a letter of intent with the Cornhuskers, not realizing that Epley was referring to him.

He signed with Nebraska, after assistant Frank Solich, the Cornhuskers' freshman coach, noticed him while watching film of a tight end from Pennsauken, New Jersey. Rozier was a fullback in a Wishbone offense, and, more importantly, he was eager to get out of Camden. The final game of his senior season, against rival Camden High, was interrupted by gunfire between rival motorcycle gangs. It was "just like the movie *Black Sunday*," Rozier told the *Lincoln Journal and Star*.

Before playing for the Cornhuskers, however, he spent a year at Coffeyville, Kansas, Community College. He hadn't met NCAA freshman eligibility requirements, in part because of a teachers strike, which delayed the start of his senior year at Camden's Woodrow Wilson High by nearly two months and prevented him from earning enough credits. His success at Coffeyville attracted more recruiting attention, but he remained loyal to Nebraska, and in August of 1981, after a thirty-four-hour bus ride, he arrived in Lincoln—at 2:00 A.M. He would have flown with his brother Guy a week earlier had he not been suffering from a cold. Air traffic controllers had begun a strike when he was ready to leave Camden and his mom didn't want him to fly. So he boarded the bus.

He started for the first time in the fifth game that season, against Colorado, rushing for 95 yards and 2 touchdowns on only 11 carries. But he was overshadowed by the play of another sophomore in his first start, quarterback Turner Gill, who threw a school-record-tying four touchdown passes. Alternating with Craig in his first season, Rozier came up just short of rushing for 1,000 yards and was chosen as the Associated Press Big Eight "Offensive Newcomer of the Year."

After a 22–15 loss to Clemson in the 1982 Orange Bowl game, he was allowed to skip a team party at a Miami country club and go home to Camden. He was homesick and considered not returning to school. And that wasn't the first time he thought about going home and staying. Earlier, the freshman coach, Frank Solich, who recruited him and would become his position coach for his senior season, had to persuade him not to leave.

Rozier returned for spring semester in 1982 and proceeded to rewrite the rushing and scoring sections of the Cornhusker record book. He rushed for forty-nine touchdowns during his career, a record that held until Eric Crouch broke it. Among his most memorable touchdown runs was officially just 2 yards, in a 42–10 victory against UCLA in 1983. However, he ran an estimated 75 to 85 yards. He gave ground on the "49-pitch," reversing his field from the east sideline to the west, setting up blocks and leaving frustrated defenders in his wake, in a run reminiscent of Bobby Reynolds against Missouri in 1950. "The percentages aren't with you on a play like that," Coach Tom Osborne said. "Nine out of ten times, you're probably not going to get there."

Sporting Chance

Mike Rozier took the opening kickoff of the Kansas State game at Manhattan, Kansas, in 1983, 4 yards deep in the end zone and started to run, only to change his mind. He stopped, stepped back into the end zone, and downed the ball. Oops. Safety. Kansas State had a 2–0 lead. "That really made me mad," Rozier told reporters afterward. His actions spoke for themselves. By halftime, he had rushed for 127 yards and 3 touchdowns, on only 13 carries. He finished with 227 rushing yards in the 51–25 victory.

But Rozier did. "He's 'Michael Heisman,' " said Fryar. "He can do anything."

Eric Crouch

During Nebraska's weekly teleconference on the Tuesday before the Missouri game in 2001, a newspaper reporter from Kansas City told Cornhusker quarterback Eric Crouch that the Missouri players had so much respect for his ability that they had "almost elevated you to a minor deity." Crouch accepted the praise with a typically modest smile. "My whole career of playing football, I've had to be real humble, not because I've been forced to be but that's the person I am," he said in response. "I just love the game. I love to go out there and compete. I have a lot of fun out there."

Eric Crouch was homegrown, coming from Omaha to become the Cornhuskers' third Heisman Trophy winner. (Courtesy Huskers Illustrated*)*

As it turned out, the "minor deity" hyperbole proved appropriate. Midway through the third quarter of the game, before a sun-splashed crowd of 64,204 in Columbia, Nebraska, faced third-down-and-8 at its own 5 yard line, protecting a lackluster 16–3 lead. Crouch called a pass, a short "out route" to the left, where two receivers, tight end Tracey Wistrom and split end Wilson Thomas, lined up. The play quickly broke down, with Crouch sensing pressure from behind. He stepped up into the pocket, slipped out of a tackle that would have resulted in a sack and a safety, and saw the green expanse of Faurot Field. As he started to run, having given up on finding either Wistrom or Thomas open, "I was trying to get as many yards as I could, trying to get to the end zone," he said.

Coach Frank Solich watched from the sideline as Crouch broke a couple of tackles, distancing himself from the line of scrimmage and eventually all of the Missouri defenders. He was 10 yards up the field, then 20 yards. "It was obvious he wasn't going to get caught from behind," said Solich. "He's got great acceleration." By the end of the run, Thomas was his closest pursuer. Dave Volk, a Cornhusker offensive tackle, heard the cheers but couldn't see what was happening and didn't know whether they were directed at Crouch or at the Tiger defenders trying to stop him. "I saw him run into a crowd of people and then I saw him run out of the crowd," Volk said.

The 95-yard touchdown run, the longest in school history, was a *SportsCenter* highlight and boosted Crouch back into a wide-open Heisman Trophy race. Only two of the top ten voter-getters in 2000, Oregon State's Ken Simonton and Northwestern's Damien Anderson, had returned. But Crouch had gotten off to a statistically modest start, after rushing for twenty touchdowns and passing for eleven as a junior.

In the next 3 games, he would rush for 341 yards and 8 touchdowns and pass for 353 yards and 3 touchdowns. Nebraska rolled to eight victories and a number three national ranking under his direction, setting the stage for a second *SportsCenter* highlight in a 20–10 upset of Oklahoma, ranked number two.

Coming Close

The Downtown Athletic Club of New York City awarded the first Heisman Trophy in 1935, though it wouldn't be named for John W. Heisman until a year later. Heisman, a successful collegiate football coach for thirty-six years, served as the Downtown Athletic Club's first athletic director.

Jay Berwanger, the trophy's first winner, didn't fare well against Nebraska, which defeated his University of Chicago team 28–7 at Lincoln to open the 1935 season. One of the Cornhuskers that day, junior Sam Francis, would finish second in the Heisman Trophy balloting in 1936.

Cornhusker nonwinning, top-ten finishers
(Winners' names are listed in parentheses)

1936 Sam Francis, fullback, second (Lawrence Kelley, Yale)

1950 Bobby Reynolds, halfback, fifth (Vic Janowicz, Ohio State)

1967 Wayne Meylan, middle guard, ninth (Gary Beban, UCLA)

1971 Jerry Tagge, quarterback, seventh (Pat Sullivan, Auburn)

1972 Rich Glover, middle guard, third (Johnny Rodgers, Nebraska)

1974 Dave Humm, quarterback, fifth (Archie Griffin, Ohio State)

1980 Jarvis Redwine, I-back, eighth (George Rogers, South Carolina)

1982 Dave Rimington, center, fifth; Mike Rozier, I-back, tenth (Herschel Walker, Georgia)

1983 Turner Gill, quarterback, fourth (Mike Rozier, Nebraska)

1994 Lawrence Phillips, I-back, eighth; Zach Wiegert, offensive tackle, ninth (Rashaan Salaam, Colorado)

1995 Tommie Frazier, quarterback, second (Eddie George, Ohio State)

On first and 10, midway through the fourth quarter of the Oklahoma game, with the Cornhuskers clinging to a precarious 13–10 lead, Crouch called "black 41 flash reverse pass," a play that had been put in during practice that week. The play was designed to take advantage of Oklahoma's defensive pursuit. I-back Thunder Collins was split wide to the left and went in motion, taking a handoff from Crouch and then pitching the ball to Mike Stuntz, who lined up wide to the right and was running back to the left. Instead of cutting up the field, however, Stuntz stopped and after hesitating as if considering his options, passed the ball to Crouch, who caught it in stride at the Sooner 39 yard line and headed for the end zone.

Despite the benefit of a slight angle, Oklahoma defensive back Derrick Strait couldn't catch the speedy Crouch. The play covered 63 yards and solidified his Heisman candidacy. "Maybe if I contributed in some small way that would make me feel good," said Stuntz, a true freshman, who'd agreed to play wide receiver his first season with the assurance he could return to quarterback as a sophomore. "But really, Eric's talent level, Eric's leadership are what's going to win it for him if he gets it." Crouch would get the Heisman Trophy, in the closest voting since 1985, to cap a record-setting career that included shoulder surgery and might have ended in frustration prior to his sophomore season.

The prep All-American from Omaha was one of two high-profile quarterbacks in Nebraska's 1997 recruiting class. The other was Bobby Newcombe from Albuquerque, New Mexico. Newcombe played wingback as a true freshman while Crouch redshirted, undergoing surgeries on his right ankle and left knee. Newcombe returned to quarterback the next season, and the two shared time with senior Monte Christo. Then during spring practice in 1999, with Christo gone, they competed with each other for the starting job. Their spirited competition continued though two-a-day practices in the fall before Solich finally settled on Newcombe after a scrimmage a week before the opening game at Iowa.

Crouch went home over the weekend and didn't return on Monday, causing Solich to make a trip to Omaha and miss a speaking engagement as well as the Big 12 coaches teleconference. Rumor had it Crouch was considering a transfer. He would deny that, however. "People were telling me, if you're not happy about being a football player, then do something else," he said looking back. The crisis was averted when Solich convinced him he would play an important role whether or not he was the starter. Two weeks later, in a 45–0 victory against California, Crouch ran for a touchdown, passed for a touchdown, and caught a touchdown pass from Newcombe, all during the second quarter. The next week, he became the starter, with Newcombe returning to wingback.

Despite his success, Crouch was approachable, signing autographs until everyone was accommodated and always with a ready smile. During the summer before his senior season, he waited tables at a restaurant in Omaha. One day a patron, never imagining a Cornhusker quarterback would be in such a position, said, "I'll tell you what, you look a lot like Eric Crouch. I bet you get that quite a bit."

"I get it more than you think," Crouch replied.

Setting the Stage

Barely twenty-four hours into 1994, the Nebraska buses pulled away from Miami's aging Orange Bowl stadium and headed back to Miami Beach. Silence accompanied the Cornhuskers as they crossed the Julia Tuttle Causeway and proceeded along Collins Avenue to team headquarters at the Sheraton Bal Harbour. During the ride Coach Tom Osborne talked with Barron Miles, a junior cornerback, about the 18–16 loss to Florida State. "This loss doesn't mean we can't come back," Osborne said, pointing out that Colorado had lost a national championship game to Notre Dame in the Orange Bowl following the 1990 season and had returned to defeat the Fighting Irish a year later for the national title. And even if they didn't make it back, he said, Miles and his teammates had no reason to hang their heads.

Nebraska had been a heavy underdog; Florida State was favored by as many as 17½ points, and national columnists, in their infinite wisdom, had spent the days leading up to the game dismissing the Cornhuskers as undeserving of a national title shot, despite an 11–0 record and a number two ranking in the polls. Florida State was number one and had been regarded by some as the best college football team ever until a 31–24 loss at Notre Dame, which lost a week later, also in South Bend, to Boston College, 41–39.

The national columnists wanted a Florida State–Notre Dame rematch in the Fiesta Bowl, and beyond that, a championship for Seminole Coach Bobby Bowden,

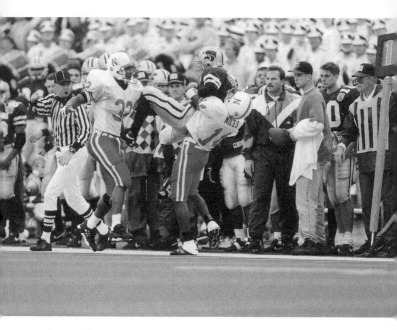

Barron Miles wraps up a Kansas State receiver as All-America line-backer Ed Stewart arrives to help. (Courtesy Huskers Illustrated)

according to Bill Vilona of the *Pensacola News Tribune*. There was a "positive sentiment among [poll] voters toward Bowden," Vilona wrote. "They want him to be number one. Right or wrong, his warm relationship with the media does have influence."

After the 18–16 loss, some Nebraska fans suggested there might have been a positive sentiment among the game officials toward Bowden as well. What would have been a 71-yard punt return for a touchdown by Cornhusker Corey Dixon was nullified by what replays seemed to indicate was a phantom clipping penalty. Then early in the second half, fullback William Floyd scored Florida State's lone touchdown despite fumbling, when officials ruled the ball had broken the plane of the goal.

Those plays were critical as Nebraska battled the Seminoles to a virtual standstill. They had led the nation in total offense and scoring, averaging 548 yards and 43.2 points per game. But Nebraska limited them to 333 yards and the 18 points—on Floyd's touchdown and 4 Scott Bentley field goals—and had a chance to win at the end. Byron Bennett missed a 45-yard field goal as time elapsed. Bennett was successful on his only other attempt, a 27-yarder, to give the Cornhuskers a 16–15 lead with 1:16 remaining.

The finish was frantic. Bentley's fourth field goal, a 22-yard chip shot, came with 21 seconds remaining, after Charlie Ward, Florida State's Heisman Trophy–winning quarterback, directed an 8-play, 60-yard drive, facilitated by a pair of 15-yard penalties against Nebraska. Ward completed 2 of 5 passes during the drive, both to freshman tailback Warrick Dunn, for 9 yards and 21 yards. Bowden elected to attempt the field goal on second and goal from the 5 yard line, with 24 seconds on the clock.

Miles returned the kickoff to his own 43-yard line, after Florida State had been assessed a 15-yard unsportsmanlike conduct penalty. Tommie Frazier threw an incomplete pass on first down but completed a second-down pass to tight end Trumane Bell for 29 yards, after which Nebraska called a timeout. The Seminoles had already dumped Gatorade on Bowden in celebration, but the officials conferred and decided to put one second back on the clock. The field had to be cleared.

Bennett, a senior from Rowlett, Texas, had earned All-Big Eight honorable mention, hitting on 6 of 11 field-goal attempts in the regular season, including 3 of 5 from 40 to

Husker Highlights

The signature play of Nebraska's 1971 national championship season was the 72-yard punt return by Johnny Rodgers against Oklahoma in the "Game of the Century." The signature play of the Cornhuskers' 1995 national championship season was Tommie Frazier's 75-yard touchdown run against Florida in the Fiesta Bowl game. Nebraska was in control and many fans in blue and orange were heading to the exits at Sun Devil Stadium when Frazier took a snap from center Aaron Graham, cut behind a block by fullback Brian Schuster, and turned up the field. The official play-by-play credited Frazier with breaking 7 tackles in the first 20 yards; no one had a chance to catch him the rest of the way. But teammate Christian Peter, a defensive lineman, claimed that Frazier had broken eleven tackles. "I counted them all," Peter said.

The signature play of Nebraska's 1997 national championship season was also the most important because without it, there would have been no championship. On the final play of regulation at Missouri, with the Cornhuskers trailing 38–31, at the Missouri 12-yard line, quarterback Scott Frost passed to split end Matt Davison for the touchdown. But it wasn't that simple. The pass was intended for wingback Shevin Wiggins, who went down to get the ball and kicked it soccer style to keep it alive. Davison, a freshman playing in only his eighth collegiate game, made a diving catch in the back of the end zone. "I was just in the right place at the right time," Davison said afterward. Kris Brown kicked the extra point for the tie and Nebraska won in overtime, 45–38. On the final play of the overtime, Cornhusker rush ends Grant Wistrom and Mike Rucker sacked Missouri quarterback Corby Jones.

Matt Davison's dramatic catch on the final play of regulation at Missouri in 1997 kept Nebraska's national championship hopes alive. (Courtesy Huskers Illustrated)

49 yards. He was five of twelve from that range during his career. Aaron Graham snapped the ball to David Seizys, who set it down. The Seminoles got a good push and penetration, Bennett told reporters afterward. "I think that altered my kick a little bit. I could just feel them." With an Orange Bowl–record crowd of 81,536 and a national television audience watching, the ball sailed wide left. And Florida State began celebrating again. Cornhusker outside linebacker Trev Alberts, who sacked Ward three times, made sure that Bennett didn't have to shoulder blame for the loss. He "did not lose the game for us, by any stretch," said Alberts, a senior cocaptain. "If we would've held them defensively, the game would've been over."

The game provided Bowden with his first national title, and Nebraska with some respect. The Cornhuskers "deserved to win it as much as we did," Bowden said. "Nebraska is a lot better than I thought." And it wasn't even full strength. Abdul Muhammad, the team's leading receiver, suffered bruised ribs on the second play of the second quarter, attempting to catch a pass from I-back Calvin Jones, and had to be taken to the hospital. Soon after, Jones, the team's leading rusher, went to the sideline with a shoulder injury. Jones, who gained 1,043 yards during the season, carried only 9 times.

More to the point, however, Nebraska was a relatively young team. Miles was among thirteen starters who would return in 1994 and make Osborne's postgame bus-ride words prophetic. The Cornhuskers would come back to the Orange Bowl and defeat Miami on its home field to earn not just Osborne's first national championship but also the first of three during his final four seasons as coach.

From that night until Osborne left the field at Miami's Pro Player Stadium—the new home of the Orange Bowl game—following his last game, a 42–17 victory against Tennessee on January 2, 1998, the Cornhuskers would lose only twice, both in 1996. They would win twenty-six in a row after the loss to Florida State, and counting 1993, their combined record over Osborne's final five seasons would be 60–3.

But that was in the future. On the morning after the Florida State loss, Osborne, operating on little sleep, met with a handful of reporters before taping his weekly coach's show at poolside at the Sheraton Bal Harbour. He told them: "A lot of people can't relate to what it means to play at a top level. They think either you're a winner or a loser. There are those who find satisfaction only in trophies and rings. But to keep playing at this level is important to me. We did everything we could. We didn't embarrass ourselves, and we played at the top level. I'm not down in the dumps. We had the snap, the hold, and the kick. But the field goal wasn't good, and there went the national championship."

The previous night's game had been Nebraska's eighth under Osborne in the Orange Bowl, and the Cornhuskers had won only once, 21–20 against LSU at the end of the 1982 season. Two other Orange Bowl losses also could have meant national championships had they been victories. And five of the games had been against either Miami or Florida State, which meant playing in front of a hostile crowd. Three were against Miami on its home field, the most notable at the end of the 1983 season, when Osborne came within a two-point conversion of winning his first national championship.

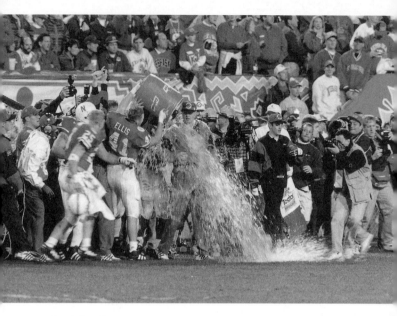

Coach Tom Osborne gets the obligatory bath, with captain Phil Ellis doing the honors, following a 62–24 victory against Coach Steve Spurrier's Florida team in the 1996 Fiesta Bowl game. Osborne's 1995 team is rated among the best in college football history. (Courtesy Huskers Illustrated)

His 1983 team, nicknamed "The Scoring Explosion," was number one in the preseason rankings and remained there through twelve games, beginning with the first Kickoff Classic. Just as Florida State would be ten years later, the 1983 Cornhuskers were regarded as college football's best ever, primarily because of the explosive offense. That explosiveness was illustrated in a 69–19 victory against Colorado, when Nebraska scored 41 points in 9 minutes and 10 seconds of the third quarter. Even more remarkable was the fact that the total time of possession was an NCAA record, two minutes and fifty-five seconds.

Nebraska proved to be vulnerable defensively, however, and number five Miami took advantage of that vulnerability, jumping out to a 17–0 first-quarter lead. The Cornhuskers battled back to tie the score early in the second half, only to see Miami pull away by the end of the third quarter, 31–17. But Nebraska came back again, even though I-back Mike Rozier, the Heisman Trophy winner, was sidelined by an ankle injury. His replacement, Jeff Smith, scored two fourth-quarter touchdowns, the second from 24 yards out on a fourth and 8 to make the score 31–30 with 48 seconds remaining.

The consensus before and after the game was that had Nebraska settled for a tie, with the extra-point kick being almost a sure thing, it would have been voted the national championship. But Osborne refused to play for a tie. Without hesitating, he called for a two-point play, a pass from quarterback Turner Gill to Smith. Miami's Ken Calhoun deflected the pass, which glanced off Smith's shoulder pads and fell incomplete. Osborne was applauded for his decision.

Ten years later, however, it had begun to look as if the 1984 Orange Bowl game was as close as Osborne would get to a national championship. The loss to Florida State in the 1994 game was Nebraska's seventh consecutive in a bowl, beginning with a 31–28 loss to the Seminoles in the 1988 Fiesta Bowl. Plus, the closest Nebraska had come in its five previous bowl games was the year before, when it also lost to the Seminoles 27–14 in the Orange Bowl. And that score probably didn't reflect the disparity.

But Nebraska's bowl trips to Florida—it also played in the 1991 Citrus Bowl in Orlando—would pay recruiting dividends. The Cornhuskers were able to attract a handful of players from the Bradenton area, most notably Frazier, the *USA Today* first-team All-America quarterback at Manatee High School. And he would be a driving force behind the national championships in 1994 and 1995. "I don't want to give the impression this is a one-man program in the last four years," Osborne said as Frazier's career was nearing an end. "But I would say if I were to choose one player who has had the most impact on the outcome of the greatest number of games over the longest period of time since I've been at Nebraska, it would be Tommie Frazier." Osborne had been at Nebraska for thirty-four years.

Frazier started six games into his freshman season and never really relinquished the job, although he missed seven games during his junior season because of a blood-clot problem, before returning to start the 24–17 Orange Bowl victory against Miami. Ironically, prior to the 1994 season, Osborne said that Frazier was the player the Cornhuskers could least afford to lose. But junior Brook Berringer stepped in at quarterback and led them to the Big Eight championship. Frazier's record as a starter was 33–3, and he was the runner-up to Ohio State's Eddie George in voting for the Heisman Trophy as a senior in 1995.

Conference rival Colorado might well have gotten Frazier. "In fact I think he had his heart and mind set on Colorado," his mom, Priscilla, told the *Omaha World-Herald*. But the Buffaloes may have lost him because of impatience. Coach Bill McCartney compared him with Kordell Stewart, the Buffaloes quarterback whose mobility allowed him to make big plays or buy time when he was looking to pass. But McCartney had targeted two other high school quarterbacks as well, Koy Detmer from Mission, Texas, and Chad Davis, a Californian who would pick

Tommie Frazier became a starter as a freshman and helped lead the Cornhuskers to national championships in 1994 and 1995. The center on those championship teams was All-American Aaron Graham (54). (Courtesy Huskers Illustrated)

Oklahoma but never earn a letter there. McCartney told Frazier and the other two that Colorado had a scholarship for the first to commit. And that was Detmer.

Frazier had plenty of other scholarship offers. The schools in Florida were interested, but he wanted to go to a program that ran an offense similar to the one at Manatee High. He wanted to run as well as pass. So he eliminated the in-state schools and made recruiting visits to Notre Dame, Clemson, and Syracuse in addition to Colorado. Nebraska was to be the last of his NCAA-allotted five official visits, but he was weary of the recruiting process by then so he considered canceling the trip. If not for his mom, he would have.

Priscilla Frazier told her son, the next-to-youngest of six children, that his word was his bond, and that if he told Nebraska he would visit, then, by golly, he had an obligation to make the visit. "I told Tommie I didn't know exactly where Nebraska was, but I was going to drag him there if I had to," she would tell the *World-Herald* later. So he made his final recruiting trip to Lincoln. "I felt he had a good visit," Osborne said on the day in early February when Frazier signed his letter of intent. The weather in Nebraska was unseasonably warm during his visit, which probably helped. "I told him it was unusually cold for this time of year," said Osborne.

Osborne and Cornhusker assistant Kevin Steele, who spent an in-home recruiting visit playing cards with Frazier and his mom, had connected with the family. During the card game with Steele, Clemson Coach Ken Hatfield stopped by in hopes of persuading Frazier to accept the Tigers' scholarship offer. When Steele left, as recruiting etiquette required, Pricilla Frazier told him to return later to finish the game.

Recruiting analysts predicted Frazier would pick either Clemson or Notre Dame. But he chose the Cornhuskers, not only because of their option offense and the fact that they had "the best chance of winning a couple of national championships," he said prophetically, but also "because they have more Academic All-Americans than anybody else and because it's a low-crime, low-pressure place to live. Besides, the people there love football, whether you win or lose, although they like winning more."

Frazier drew immediate comparisons with Turner Gill, who set the standard for Cornhusker quarterbacks in the early 1980s. Appropriately enough, Gill had just returned to coach the quarterbacks. Frazier resembled him more in presence than in style. "Tommie has always been confident in his ability. He has high self-esteem," said Tyrone Williams, a friend and teammate since elementary school who also came to Nebraska and started at cornerback on the 1994–95 national championship teams. "He's not one to follow."

That was apparent from his first season. No true freshman had ever started at quarterback for Osborne. Gill hadn't started until the fifth game of his sophomore season. But by the sixth game in 1992, Frazier felt he was ready. "You never know how well a guy is going to pick things up," said Osborne. "Tommie probably picked up things quicker than anybody we've ever had. He was exceptional." In that first start, against Missouri at Columbia, Frazier played all but one series and scored three touchdowns in a 34–24 victory. Afterward, he declined interview requests. He didn't want to draw attention from his teammates, he told the sports information office, in particular the seniors. That was his approach. He couldn't control what others said about him, but he could control what he said about himself.

Nebraska finished 1992 with a 9–3 record and out of the top ten for a fourth consecutive season. But Frazier's leadership and ability to run Osborne's option offense were reasons for optimism. The team's Unity Council adopted the theme "Refuse to Lose" for the 1993 season and had it printed on T-shirts that players wore under their pads. They were ranked number nine in the first Associated Press poll.

Their climb in the rankings was slow. They trailed in four of eleven regular-season games and were tied or ahead by no more than a touchdown in the fourth quarter of seven games. By late October they were fifth in the AP poll, but they dropped to sixth after a 49–7 victory against Missouri and remained there for two weeks, despite defeating number twenty Colorado at Boulder, 21–17, in a game that showed Frazier's grit.

The Cornhuskers started fast, taking a 21–3 first-quarter lead before Colorado's defense settled down. The Buffaloes cut the deficit to 21–10 at halftime, and on the second play from scrimmage in the second half, when he was brought down at the end of a 26-yard run, Frazier suffered a sprain of his right shoulder. Five minutes later, however, he returned. His presence in the huddle gave the offense an emotional boost, said Dixon, who had teamed with Frazier on a 60-yard touchdown pass in the first quarter. "He was hurting."

The pain was excruciating in fact, and after two series, he took himself out, went to the locker room, where the shoulder was x-rayed, then went back out to watch the fourth quarter from the sideline, wrapped in a heavy cape to protect against thirty-degree temperatures and snowballs hurled from the Colorado student section. Some sixty people were escorted out of the stadium during the game for throwing the snowballs, which were easily made. A heavy snow had been cleared from the field that morning.

Even with Frazier, Nebraska's offense sputtered, as did Colorado's. Neither team could score in the third quarter. But under the direction of Stewart, the Buffaloes put together a 15-play, 80-yard touchdown drive, finished off by Rashaan Salaam with 2:54 remaining. While Colorado was driving, Frazier talked to Osborne about going back into the game if the Buffaloes scored. He wouldn't run the risk of further injuring the shoulder by playing. The only consideration was the pain. He couldn't raise his right arm above his head without wincing, but "if I'm able to go out there and perform at 75 percent, I'm going to go out there and do it," he said afterward. "It's one of those mind over matter things."

The Cornhuskers still needed an interception of a Stewart pass at their own 30 yard line with 1:21 remaining to wrap up their eighth victory. But Frazier had shown his teammates he would do whatever he could to help them win. "We knew Tommie has a lot of heart," said Dixon.

Nebraska would escape with one-point victories twice during the 1993 season, 14–13 against UCLA at the Rose Bowl at Pasadena in the third game and 21–20 against Kansas at Lawrence the week after the Colorado game. And both times the Alberts-led defense came up big. Early in the fourth quarter of the UCLA game, the Bruins had a first down at the Nebraska 14 yard line, trailing 14–10. But the defense held, forcing them to settle for a field goal. They would pick up only one first down and never get beyond their 26 yard line the rest of the way.

On a sunny but cold afternoon in Lawrence, the Jayhawks held Nebraska in check and had an opportunity to win with a two-point conversion after scoring a touchdown

Coming Up Roses

Through the 2003 season, Nebraska had played in thirty-five consecutive bowl games, beginning with the 1969 team's trip to the Sun Bowl. Cornhusker fans have come to expect postseason play. But prior to 1962 and the arrival of Coach Bob Devaney—whose teams went to nine bowls in eleven seasons—Nebraska had made only two bowl appearances. The second has been forgotten, or at least ignored. The Cornhuskers represented the Big Seven in the 1955 Orange Bowl game because the conference had a no-repeat rule. Champion Oklahoma couldn't go, so runner-up Nebraska did—and lost to Duke 34–7.

Nebraska's first bowl game, however, was held in such esteem, Devaney often joked, that he had been the Cornhuskers coach for some time before finding out Coach "Biff" Jones's Cornhuskers had lost to Stanford in the 1941 Rose Bowl game. The New Year's Day game drew a record crowd of 92,000, and the *Omaha World-Herald* estimated that as many as 30,000 were Nebraskans.

After the announcement that Nebraska had accepted an invitation to play in the Rose Bowl, the celebration in Lincoln lasted more than twenty-four hours, according to Lincoln newspaper accounts, with celebrants packing city streets. The Cornhuskers had lost their opening game in 1940 to perennial power Minnesota, 13–7, and then won eight in a row to earn the invitation. The team was home-grown. Of the forty-three players who made the trip, forty-two were from Nebraska. One was from Kansas. And though they lost, 21–13, there was no disgrace. "Here's a bunch of plow jockeys who could keep up with the big city boys," Herm Rohrig would recall years later. Rohrig played tailback in Nebraska's single-wing offense. Coach Clark Shaughnessy's Stanford team operated out of an innovative T formation, directed by quarterback Frankie Albert.

that made the score 21–20 with 52 seconds remaining. Nebraska defensive coordinator Charlie McBride expected a run to the outside because that's how the Jayhawks had been successful. Freshman June Henley had gained 148 yards on 37 carries behind a big offensive line that had worn down the defense. So McBride called a two-man blitz, with one coming from each side. Because of a miscommunication, however, both blitzers came from the same side, and Kansas quarterback Asheiki Preston rolled out in the opposite direction, looking to pass. With Cornhusker defensive tackle Kevin Ramaekers in pursuit, Preston threw into the end zone. But the pass fell short of the intended receiver. Henley hadn't even been in the game. Watching the play unfold left him with a helpless feeling, Alberts said afterward, "We were pretty lucky today."

The Cornhuskers could have used some of that luck against Florida State in the Orange Bowl game. They took the lucky horseshoe that hung above the double doors leading from the locker room to the playing field at Memorial Stadium with them to Miami, where they hung it on the locker room wall there. But the night before game, the horseshoe fell off the wall, an omen of things to come.

As Osborne told Miles, however, they had no reason to hang their heads. Osborne had a special affection for the 1993 team. It was "awfully good," he said after he retired from coaching. "I thought we played at the national championship level. I think the '93 team has to go down as one of the best."

It set the stage for what was to happen. "We come back next year and get it going and play for the national championship here again," Frazier said after the 18–16 loss. And that's exactly what happened.

About the Author

Mike Babcock is a freelance writer, working primarily as a contributing editor for *Huskers Illustrated*. He also writes about the Cornhuskers for the *Grand Island Independent*, *York News-Times* and *Columbus Telegram*. He spent seventeen of twenty-six years covering Nebraska football at the *Lincoln Journal Star* and has written several books, including *Go Big Red: The Ultimate Fan's Guide to Nebraska Cornhusker Football*, *The Nebraska Football Legacy*, *Tom Osborne: An Era of Excellence*, and *Huskers on the Hardwood: 100 Years of University of Nebraska Basketball*. He also collaborated on *Devaney: By Bob Devaney (and Friends)*. A native of York, Nebraska, Babcock has two children, Chad and Heather, and lives with wife Barb and two cats, Garcia and Bear, in Lincoln, Nebraska.